SHEFFIELD HALLAM UNIVERSITY
LEA
COLLEGIAT
SHE

D1434424

101 795 951 X

ONE V

Sheffield Hallam University
Learning and Information Services
Withdrawn From Stock

The Nation in History

THE NATION
in HISTORY

Historiographical Debates about

Ethnicity and Nationalism

Anthony D. Smith

POLITY PRESS

Copyright © 2000 by the Historical Society of Israel

First published in the United Kingdom in 2000 by Polity Press in association with Blackwell Publishers Ltd

Simultaneously published in the United States of America by University Press of New England, Hanover, NH

Editorial office:
Polity Press
65 Bridge Street
Cambridge CB2 1UR, UK

Marketing and Production:
Blackwell Publishers Ltd
108 Cowley Road
Oxford OX4 1 JF, UK

All rights reserved. Except for the quotation of short passages for the purposes of criticism and review, no part of this publication may be reproduced, stored in a retrieval system, or transmitted, in any form or by any means, electronic, mechanical, photocopying, recording or otherwise, without the prior permission of the publisher.

Except in the United States of America, this book is sold subject to the condition that it shall not, by way of trade or otherwise, be lent, re-sold, hired out, or otherwise circulated without the publisher's prior consent in any form of binding or cover other than that in which it is published and without a similar condition including this condition being imposed on the subsequent purchaser.

The lectures were originally presented under the auspices of the Historical Society of Israel, the Menahem Stern Jerusalem Lectures.

ISBN 0-7456-2580-0 (pbk)

A catalogue record for this book is available from the British Library.

This book is printed on acid-free paper.

SHEFFIELD HALLAM UNIVERSITY
WL
320.54
SM
COLLEGIATE CRESCENT

Contents

Foreword

Yosef Kaplan

In a few weeks we shall mark the tenth anniversary of the tragic death of our teacher and friend Menahem Stern. Once again we shall go up to the cemetery on Har Hamenuhot in Jerusalem, as we have done every year; again we shall recite those eternal words from the Psalms; and again we shall feel as if the author of those sublime verses were referring to Stern's spirit when he wrote: "Oh, how I love your teachings! They are my meditation all day long. . . . I have kept my feet from every evil way, so that I might keep your word" (Ps. 119:97, 101).

It was easy to love Menahem Stern, and indeed he was beloved by everyone who had the privilege of knowing him. He was a man of peace in the full meaning of the term, a humanist with his entire heart and soul, who never allowed even a hint of hatred to stain his behavior, his way of life, and his humanistic worldview.

His life was cut short in Jerusalem, the city to which he was bound with all the cords of his heart, by blind hatred that was entirely foreign to his personality and his *exemplar humanae vitae.*

In establishing the Jerusalem Lectures in History in Memory of Menahem Stern six years ago, the Historical Society of Israel wished to express the feelings of esteem and obligation of the community of historians in Israel to the greatest scholar of Jewish history during the Second Temple period in our generation and one of the most prominent scholars ever produced by the field of Jewish studies. In this way we wished to honor the memory and intellectual legacy of a brilliant historian who, from the start of his studies at the Hebrew University in Jerusalem in 1943 until his death, never interrupted his historical research, not

Opening address to Professor Anthony D. Smith's Jerusalem Lectures in History in Memory of Menahem Stern, 11 May 1999.

even for a single day; a historian of astounding erudition, whose knowledge was not restricted to specific periods or fields but who felt at home in all periods of Jewish history and no less so in classical and European cultures.

Nationalism played a central role in Menahem Stern's life. Identification with the rebirth of the Jewish nation brought his parents to the Land of Israel a short time before the outbreak of the Second World War. Stern was then thirteen years old, a talented boy from a Yiddish-speaking family in Bialystock, where he absorbed not only the riches of the ancient Jewish heritage but also the foundations of modern Hebrew culture. When he became a historian, he gave expression, throughout his academic career and in his extensive scholarship, to his deep commitment to the renewal of Hebrew culture, which is one of the outstanding marks of modern Jewish nationalism. To our great regret, nationalism, in its dark aspect, also played a role in his death.

He had reservations about the name "The Jerusalem School," which was applied to the group of historians who laid the guidelines for research in Jewish history at the Hebrew University in Jerusalem and to the first generation of their students, to which Stern belonged. At the same time, he realized that these historians and he himself shared a national approach to Jewish history. Menahem Stern was one of the five Jerusalem historians who collaborated in writing the comprehensive *History of the Jewish People*, edited by Haim Hillel Ben-Sasson. It was clear to him that a definition applicable to those five historians, "despite the great differences among them, would take into account their inclination to describe Jewish history as the history of a living nation . . . including the various aspects of its life, and not, emphatically, the history of Judaism."[1] There is no doubt that his own work was deeply influenced by the perennialist approach to Jewish history and to the Jewish nation, which was one of the distinguishing features of the historiographical view of those who founded the study of Jewish history in Israel.

In the general introduction to the Hebrew edition of the *History of the Jewish People*, which was published in 1969 (interestingly, that introduction was not published in the English edition that came out in 1976), Ben-Sasson wrote: "The national framework is still appropriate for the true clarification of history, for it is the natural and conscious framework that organizes generation after generation of human actions and social relations."[2] Ben-Sasson added:

The continued existence of one nation out of many is a series of transformations within the framework of unifying factors and forces. The Jewish nation has recorded one of the oldest continuous histories in the world. The proper study of the history of this nation shows that in the movement and dispersal of the Jews throughout their long and varied history, there is far more continuity in the body that bears the culture, far more preservation of symbols of unity and solidarity, and far more persistence of culture than among most of the nations by whose side and in whose shadow the Jews lived.[3]

Though there are good reasons to suppose that Stern was not entirely in agreement with some of these statements, there is no doubt that his work also belongs to the category of "continuous perennialism," as defined by Anthony Smith; and in Stern's relation to the Zealots and Sicarii, whom he defined as "branches of a national liberation movement," one can find something resembling the retrospective nationalism that characterized the work of more than a few historians of Ancient Israel and of scholars of Jewish history from the Hasmonean period to the Bar-Kokhba uprising.[4]

The study of Jewish history has expanded since then, and historiographical controversies have arisen around the question of the continuity of Jewish history, the place of nationalism in it, and so on. The influence of national ideology on Jewish historiography here in Israel has declined since then, for the same reasons that the old belief in the unity and superiority of the nation has declined in the contemporary West, and of course for other reasons as well, which are peculiar to our experience here in Israel. The penetrating discussions that take place in Israeli society regarding national and cultural identity naturally echo within academic discussions of continuity and change in Jewish history and of the connection between modern Jewish nationalism and Jewishness in premodern periods. This is not surprising, though, in this controversy, regrettably, we often lack the modesty of which Stern spoke and that was so typical of his scholarship. In these heated arguments, which are naturally imbued with political and ideological assumptions, imprecise concepts are frequently aired; this does not favor the clarification of issues, which demands more than a little self-restraint.

Therefore, we could not hope for a more appropriate lecturer at this time than Professor Anthony Smith, who is one of the major scholars of ethnicity and nationalism during the past thirty years. With the appearance of the first edition of his *Theories of Nationalism* in 1971, he emerged as one of the central theoreticians in the study of nationalism. One after another he has published an impressive series of articles and books that are regarded as landmarks in the study of nationalism. These include *Nationalism in the Twentieth Century* (1979), *The Ethnic Revival in the Modern World* (1981), *The Ethnic Origins of Nations* (1986), *National Identity* (1991), *Nations and Nationalism in a Global Era* (1995), and most recently, *Nationalism and Modernism* (1998).

Many of us historians engage in dialogue with the disciplines of social science, both to sharpen the conceptual and theoretical aspects of our historical research and also to add historical and cultural depth to the works of sociologists, anthropologists, and other social scientists. It is to Anthony Smith's credit that this dialogue is an integral part of his work, which is outstanding in its conceptual sharpness and rich theoretical imagination, on the one hand, and in extensive historical knowledge and understanding, on the other.

While it is possible to find clear continuity in his writing and a consistent search for the connection between preexistent ethnicity and modern nationalism, it is also characterized by the tireless quest for a unified theory or agreed paradigm that will encompass all the problems and topics included within nationalism. As a student of Ernest Gellner, his point of departure was acceptance of the modernity of both nations and nationalism. In his recent work he has also emphasized that "the modernists are surely right to insist on the modernity of *many* nations as well as of nationalism-in-general (the ideology and theory). The conditions of modernity clearly favour the replication of nations, national states and nationalism in all parts of the globe."[5]

However, the transition that took place in his scholarly interest—from nationalism to nations and from nations to ethnic communities—brought him to appreciate the important role played by ethnicity in the ancient and medieval world and the immense power contained in ethnic survival. Hence, he came to the conclusion that "the problem of ethnic survival seemed particularly important for later nationalisms: the ability to call on a rich and well documented 'ethno-history' was to prove a major cultural resource for nationalists."[6] Moreover: "Specific nations are also the product of older, often premodern ethnic ties and ethnohistories."[7] Or, in an even sharper formulation: "Some nations and their particular nationalisms have existed well before the advent of modernity."[8]

In his penetrating and extraordinarily interesting controversy with the theses of Hobsbawm and Anderson, Smith argued: "The 'inventions' of modern nationalists must resonate with large numbers of the designated 'co-nationals,' otherwise the project will fail. If they are not perceived as 'authentic' . . . they will fail to mobilise them for political action. Better, then, to 'rediscover' and reappropriate an ethnic past or pasts that mean something to the people in question, and so reconstruct anew an existing ethnic identity, even where it appears shadowy and ill documented."[9]

Smith is far from any sense that he has resolved all the complicated problems aroused by the issue of nationalism. Only recently he has said that "the analysis of nationalism remains elusive. So many basic questions continue unanswered, so few scholars are prepared to agree even on first principles."[10]

Dear Anthony Smith, who more than we, as Israelis, for whom the intense project of building a national culture in which new and old are mingled is our daily bread, is aware of the complexity and difficulty of understanding the national phenomenon. Who more than we, who are involved in Jewish history over the ages, are aware of the complexity of the questions regarding continuity and change that a concept such as "nation" arouses, which, as you noted so well, is firmly embedded historically. We thank you for coming to share your knowledge and thoughts with us. We can only hope that you will find compensation for your trouble and effort in this renewed encounter with the questions and insights that our life here in the State of Israel will again raise in the mind of an intellectual steeped in curiosity like yourself.

Acknowledgments

For some years I had been preoccupied with the question of the historical nature of the category of the nation and of the antiquity of particular nations like the Greeks, Armenians, Persians and Jews. So I was especially pleased to receive an invitation from the Historical Society of Israel to give the 1999 Jerusalem Lectures in memory of Professor Menahem Stern on the subject of "The Nation in History." As I had only been able to touch on these issues in previous publications, this invitation gave me the opportunity to develop my views in the context of the many debates among historians of ethnicity and nationalism. This book is an extended version of the Jerusalem lectures.

I should like to record my great appreciation and gratitude to the Society, and in particular to its chairman, Professor Yosef Kaplan, and his colleagues, Professors Jonathan Frankel and Michael Heyd, for their warm welcome, kindness and hospitality. I should also like to thank them for the chance to meet with a group of Israeli doctoral students in history and to discuss their research with them. I am particularly grateful to Mr. Zvi Yekutiel, General Secretary of the Historical Society of Israel, to Ma'ayan Avineri-Rebhun and to Tovi Weiss for their care and attention to my needs and those of my family, both before and during my visit, and for making our stay both enjoyable and rewarding.

Finally, I would like to express my thanks to University Press of New England and to April Ossmann for publishing these lectures, and for seeing the manuscript through to publication with such speed and efficiency.

London School of Economics   A.D.S.
October 1999

The Nation in History

Introduction

I was greatly honored to have been invited by the Historical Society of Israel to deliver the 1999 lectures in memory of the late Professor Stern. This is doubly the case, first, because of his eminence in the field of Hellenistic Jewish history and, second, because my own first love was ancient history, in particular the history of Israel and the classical world, the very field in which Professor Stern made such a distinguished contribution before his tragic death. My thoughts have returned more than once to this seminal period of ancient and Jewish history in order to gain some perspective on the problems of ethnicity and nationalism. I was therefore particularly grateful to the society for their kind invitation to lecture in Jerusalem.

My theme is a large one, the role of the nation and nationalism in history. It is a theme that has attracted considerable attention and debate among historians and social scientists. Given the many disputes in the field, the topic must be approached indirectly, through an investigation of the historiography of nationalism and of the many histories of the nation proferred by scholars. In what follows, I am concerned mainly with the theoretical debates among the historians of nationalism. But given the interdisciplinary nature of the field and the influence of scholars in neighboring disciplines on the approaches and formulations of historians, I must also consider the work of political scientists, sociologists, anthropologists, and others who have contributed to the fundamental debates on the role of ethnicity and nationalism. I need hardly add that, in the short time at my disposal, I can give only a very general, synoptic view of the many contributions to this vast and rapidly advancing field.

The successive histories of nations and nationalism are not simply products of various historians' outlooks and situations nor even of different national situations and historical traditions, relevant though these often are. They are explicable mainly in terms of the historians' engagement in certain fundamental "paradigm debates," which have defined and still define the understanding and study of these phenomena. These debates center on three issues:

1. the nature and origin of the nation and nationalism,
2. the antiquity or modernity of nations and nationalism,
3. the role of nations and nationalism in historical and especially recent social change.

Each of these central issues is understood and treated differently by historians and social scientists, adhering to rival paradigms of nations and nationalism. As a result, the changing historiography of the field is largely the history of the characterization, periodization, and historical role definition of nations and nationalism in terms of these conflicting paradigms.

Hence my starting point is that there can be no single "history of the nation" or of nationalism, but neither is there an infinite number of such histories. What we have instead is a finite number of competing histories determined in large part by the historiographical debates generated by rival paradigms for understanding and explaining the character, historical location, and social and political role of nations and nationalism. This formulation should not be understood as yet another assertion of a fashionable "social constructionism." It is, rather, a recognition of the way in which social theory molds historical perceptions and definitions of nations and nationalism and their role in history. "Theory" here signifies both an overall philosophy of history and a more specific historical sociology of culture and politics; and it is these underlying theoretical assumptions that concern me in this analysis of the main historiographical debates about nationalism—as much as any understanding of the origins, location, and role of particular nations and nationalisms.[1]

Three fundamental debates have structured and continue to define the historiography of nationalism:

1. The organicist versus the voluntarist understanding of the na-

tion and the contemporary debates between primordialists and instrumentalists that stem from these understandings.

2. The perennialist versus the modernist approaches to nations and nationalism and the contemporary debates about the antiquity or modernity of nations.

3. The social constructionist versus the ethnosymbolic approaches to nations and nationalisms and the contemporary debates about the relationship of the past and present in the formation and future of nations.

From these debates we can isolate and describe four main paradigms of understanding of nations and nationalism: the primordialist, the perennialist, the modernist, and the ethnosymbolic paradigms. They account for most of the contributions to the key historiographical debates.[2] Now, each of these paradigms proposes quite different understandings of the character, role, and formation of nations and nationalisms, and in doing so, subscribes to very different definitions of the key terms, *nation* and *nationalism*. Hence, before embarking on an analysis of the rival paradigms and debates, I need to indicate my own understandings and working definitions of these terms as a benchmark for comparison with competing definitions.

By the term *nation*, I understand *a named human population occupying a historic territory or homeland and sharing common myths and memories; a mass, public culture; a single economy; and common rights and duties for all members*. By the term *nationalism*, I understand *an ideological movement for the attainment and maintenance of autonomy, unity, and identity on behalf of a population deemed by some of its members to constitute an actual or potential "nation."*[3]

It is important to stress that these are working definitions and that, like all definitions, they are embedded within a more general perspective or paradigm. To this view and its theoretical paradigm I shall return later. It is one that has emerged out of the criticisms and limitations of the dominant modernist paradigm and, in particular, in opposition to its "constructionist" variant. This means it can be approached only through an analysis of the modernist paradigm. But since the modernist paradigm in turn responded to earlier theoretical paradigms, it is necessary to push the analysis a stage further back, to the first formulations of historians who sought to analyze the rising tide of nationalism in Europe.

Hence, the format of my present discussion follows the logic and chronology of the basic theoretical paradigms and the debates they have generated. Historically, the earliest of these debates concerned the organic or voluntary character of nations and nationalisms. For this reason I begin by examining the historical roots of the first major paradigm, the organic and historicist paradigm, and the associated contemporary debates about the primordial character of the nation. My aim here is twofold: to reveal the significance as well as the drawbacks of an organic and primordialist paradigm and, at the same time, to show that, though there is a clear normative distinction between these competing conceptions of the nation, most historical cases reveal varying mixtures of civic and ethnic elements.

Equally important is the second major paradigm debate, which concerns the historical periodization of nations and nationalism. Here I am concerned to scrutinize the dominant modernist paradigm that emerged after the Second World War in opposition to a much earlier perennialist perspective. In many ways, the debate about the antiquity or modernity of nations and nationalism forms the core of historiographical discussion and disagreements, and it has received new impetus from recent perennialist challenges to modernist orthodoxy. But it would appear that, despite their often insightful criticisms, the various versions of perennialism are unable to offer sufficient evidence, except in a very few instances, to undermine the basic modernist paradigm of nations and nationalism.

Recently, we have seen a trend that seeks to go beyond modernism by demonstrating the specific context of nations and nationalism and hence the need to deconstruct and transcend both in a globalizing era. Such postmodern "social constructionism" has provoked considerable debate; and partly in response to its claims, some scholars are seeking to reestablish the historical embeddedness of nations in prior ethnic and cultural formations and the need to examine the ethnosymbolic genealogies of modern nations over the *longue durée*. I hope to show that an ethnosymbolic perspective can offer a more comprehensive and potentially richer understanding of the complex historical role of nations and nationalism than its rivals can.

1 Voluntarism and the Organic Nation

The term *primordialism* is fairly recent, and it is used in a variety of ways, often pejoratively. In general terms it refers to the idea that certain cultural attributes and formations possess a prior, overriding, and determining influence on people's lives, one that is largely immune to "rational" interest and political calculation. We are, in a certain sense, compelled by the attachments that spring from these attributes and formations. They stand apart from, and often above, the rational choices and the pursuit of material interests that characterize much of our lives. Among these attachments, those deriving from such cultural attributes as kinship and descent, language, religion, and customs, as well as historical territory, assume a prominent place; they tend to give rise to that sense of communal belonging we call ethnicity and ethnic community; and they form the basis for the subsequent development of nations and nationalism. For these reasons, nations and nationalisms possess a special character and occupy a privileged place in history; in this sense, they can be termed primordial, existing, as it were, before history, in nature's "first order of time."[1]

There is no single version of primordialism, as there is no single version of modernism or perennialism. But we can distinguish three broad strands or versions: an organicist, a sociobiological, and a cultural primordialism. I shall say very little here about the sociobiological version because, despite its recent revival, it has not made a noticeable impact on current historiographical debates. Eric Hobsbawm makes some play with a possible genetic meaning of ethnicity, but in general no historian of nationalism appears to have taken up the sociobiological or neo-Darwinian challenge. Cultural primordialism, on the other hand, has been more influential in recent years, and I shall return to it later. For the moment I want to concentrate on the most familiar and widespread version of primordialism, namely, organicism—or more precisely, the historicist and organic conception of nationalism—for this was the earliest version of primordialism and the most influential on subsequent historical theorizing in this field.[2]

Organic and Voluntarist Nationalism

It was Hans Kohn, in his influential *The Idea of Nationalism* ([1944] 1967a), written at the height of the Second World War, who drew attention to the differences between two ideological versions of nationalism: the voluntarist and the organic. In his typology, voluntarist or associational forms of nationalism were prevalent in the West, that is to say, west of the Rhine—in France, the Low Countries, and especially Britain and America. Conversely, organic forms of nationalism were dominant in Central and Eastern Europe, Russia, the Middle East, and much of Asia. The two kinds of nationalism displayed a number of contrasting features, but the basic opposition concerned the relationship of the individual to the collectivity. In both kinds of nationalism the individual must belong to a nation; there is no chance of surviving outside the bond of the nation. But in the voluntaristic type, the individual can, in principle, choose to which nation she or he wishes to belong; in that limited sense, the nation is a contractual political association. A voluntarist ideal of the nation guarantees the right of individuals to choose their nation of belonging. In contrast, organic versions of nationalism reject any such right. The individual is born into a nation, and is indelibly stamped with its character and genius for life. Migrate where he or she may, the individual always retains his or her nationality of birth.

For Kohn, this basic contrast generated other oppositions. In the voluntarist version, the nation is regarded as a rational territorial association of citizens: the members are bound together by laws based on a contract freely entered into, and they come to form a political community living according to a single code of laws and sharing a single political culture in a recognized historic territory. By contrast, in the organic version of nationalism, the nation is conceived of as a spiritual principle and as a seamless whole transcending the individual members; the members are bound together by a myth of common origins and a shared historic culture, and they form a single cultural community living according to vernacular codes in a historic homeland.[3]

The contrast between the two kinds of nationalism Hans Kohn explained in both social and geopolitical terms. A voluntarist and civic-political nationalism required a strong, rational bourgeoisie to act as a "bearer class" in the task of building and leading the mass citizen-nation, just as it also needed the competition of roughly equal states to ensure the necessary stability, liberties, and powers of the bourgeois property owners. In contrast, an organic nationalism normally appears in the absence of a strong bourgeoisie and interstate competition. We find it, argued Kohn, in the agrarian lands of the East, dominated by semifeudal landowners and ruled by imperial autocrats. Here the national movement is led by a small urban intelligentsia; and in the absence of wider support it acquires a shrill, authoritarian tone and often a mystical character (Kohn [1944] 1967a, 329–31; Kohn 1955).

Now, Kohn's celebrated dichotomy did not emerge in a vacuum. It drew on and systematized a long tradition of often invidious classification of nations and nationalism, a tradition that can be traced back to the late eighteenth century and more specifically to Herder's break with Enlightenment rationalism and his adoption of what Sir Isaiah Berlin terms a "cultural populism." However, at the beginning of the eighteenth century, ideas of distinctive national character already had taken root, expressed in such notions as the "genius of the nation" of Lord Shaftesbury, Boullainvilliers's defense of the Franks against the Gauls, Bolingbroke's conjunction of patriotism and freedom, Vico's cultural historicism of successive nations, and Montesquieu's *esprit général de la nation* (Kemilainen 1964; Berlin 1979, 99–110; Llobera 1994, 151–57).[4]

But it was only in Rousseau's later writings that the fundamental contrasts between naturalism and voluntarism and between culture and politics began to emerge. Earlier, Rousseau had subscribed to the general Enlightenment belief in the nation as a contractual or voluntary association dedicated to liberty and justice. But by the 1760s he began to impart to this rationalist ideal a new emotional fervor and religious zeal. On the one hand, Rousseau assumed the givenness of nationality—the existence of nations, as the Abbé Siéyès later put it, "in the state of nature."

On the other hand, he preached to the recently liberated Corsicans in 1765 the need to cultivate the Spartan and stoic virtues of courage, agrarian simplicity, and a life of harmony with nature, which would enable them to create a sense of nationhood; and to Poles in 1772, the need to retain and cultivate, through a program of national education and rituals, their cultural heritage of language, games, festivals, and customs in order to preserve a distinct Polish nation, which was then in the throes of being dismembered in the Partitions. (See Kohn [1944] 1967a, 237–59; Llobera 1994, 157–64; Cohler 1970.)

In similar vein, Rousseau praised lawgivers like Moses, Lycurgus, and Numa Pompilius for their wisdom and farsightedness in creating separate moral communities through a strict code of laws and a dense network of rituals. Of the Mosaic Law, he wrote: "Through it alone that extraordinary nation, so often subjugated, so often dispersed and outwardly destroyed, but always idolatrous of its Law, has preserved itself unto our days, scattered among the others, but never confounded with them. Its mores, laws and rituals persist and will persist to the end of the world, despite the hatred and persecution of the rest of mankind" (J-J.Rousseau: *Oeuvres completes* 2:786, cited in Baron 1960, 26–27).[5]

This fundamental tension between collective will and received culture, between contractual lawmaking and collective character and tradition, is succinctly expressed in Rousseau's dictum: "The first rule that we must follow is that of national character. Every people has, or must have, a character; if it lacks one, we must begin by endowing it with one" (Rousseau 1915, 2:319, *Project Corse*).

This suggests that Rousseau recognized the received basis of society in the preexisting bonds of peoplehood and culture or "national character." For Rousseau, in the words of F. M. Barnard, "Nation-building . . . is not simply a matter of national purpose and political will. To be a nation requires continuity as well as identity, a tradition of culture as well as the creation of a political structure" (Barnard 1983, 239).

At the same time, Rousseau thought it possible, and vital, to rectify or improve that character by legislation and national education. It is not walls nor people that make *la patrie*, he contends; "it is the laws, the mores, the customs, the government, the constitution, and the mode of existence that results from all these.

The *patrie* exists in the relations of the State to its members; when those relations change, or perish, the *patrie* vanishes" (J.-J. Rousseau, *Correspondance générale*, ed. T. Dufour [Paris, Colin 1924–34] 10:337–38, cited in Kohn [1944] 1967a, 659 n. 113; see also Cohler 1970).

This dualism of nature and civilization, culture and political will, resonates through the early attempts to make sense of and evaluate the effects of nationalism. For Herder, too, despite the large role that he gives to culture and language and the importance that he confers on authentic group experience, there remains an important element of civilization and even will. Men and women should, after all, *choose* to follow their own path, speak their own language, rediscover their own history, and "think their own thoughts." "Let men think well or ill of us; they are our language, our literature, our ways, and let that be enough" (cited in Berlin 1976, 182).

Certainly, Herder proclaims the moral equality of cultures and the need to immerse oneself in one's own history and culture if one is to be truly free. It is part of God's plan that we experience the world in organic groups, that the "people" are the natural repository of authentic experience, and that vernacular language and culture are the authentic expressions of our collective identity and experience. In these respects, Herder's influence undoubtedly contributed significantly to the spread of an organic and historicist view of nations. But Herder also sees this providential plan as furthering the generic process of education, enlightenment, and individual self-improvement, of that ideal of *Bildung*, which was the goal of Enlightenment thinkers throughout Europe. Hence, the contrast between Herder's *volkish* "cultural populism" and Rousseau's emphasis on law, liberty, and the collective will should not be overdrawn. If there was a naturalistic dimension in Rousseau's vision, the Enlightenment's civic ideals were shared by Herder; but he sought to base them on a different, more historicist and organic—and therefore, in his view, more solidaristic—foundation than the neoclassical or Spartan political ideal of the more stoic *philosophes* (Berlin 1976; Barnard 1965).

The tension between this historicist and organic culturalism and the political voluntarism that can be discerned in the writings of the founding fathers of nationalism was accentuated in the work of their immediate and later followers: Fichte, Muller,

Arndt, and Jahn in Germany, Mazzini in Italy, and Michelet in France. Fichte and the other German Romantics gave Herder's organic culturalism a specifically political dimension by arguing that true freedom consists in the absorption of individual self-determining wills in the collective Will of the community or the state. This was to be achieved by the correct determination of individual wills through a process of national education in the vernacular language. Only through education and national struggle could individuals realize their authentic selves in the national self. Here too, nature is mingled with deliberate nurture, and the national will is formed through striving for authenticity. (See Reiss 1955; Kedourie 1960, chap. 3.)[6]

In this way, historicism and the organic analogy were always being tempered by voluntaristic elements; and political intervention was commended wherever nature seemed to fall short of the political ideal. So in policy prescriptions as well as theoretical analyses, an organic and historicist concept of the nation was always being supplemented, and thereby undercut, by a voluntaristic and civic nationalism that aimed to create the nations that were assumed to be underlying elements of nature. Nationalism, which we defined as "an ideological movement to attain and maintain autonomy, unity, and identity on behalf of a population deemed by some of its members to constitute an actual or potential 'nation,'" was, like a latter-day Prince Charming, always seeking to rediscover the submerged and forgotten nation and, in doing so, was creating the very nations whose hidden existence it assumed (Minogue 1967; Pearson 1993).

Cultural Determinism and the Political Ideal

Nevertheless, these tensions and contradictions in the very concept of the nation and between that concept and the practice of nationalism did not become subjects for scholarly historical analysis until the latter half of the nineteenth century. It was really only after 1848 and particularly after the Franco-Prussian War of 1870, that these tensions became apparent to historians, who were themselves often closely involved in the rediscovery and authentication of the national past, fueling a debate that was as much political as intellectual. It was in the light of the subsequent bitter dispute over the lands of Alsace and Lorraine that Ernest Renan delivered his celebrated lecture in 1882, entitled *Qu'est-ce qu'une nation?*, which has become the *locus classicus* of a political and voluntaristic conception of the nation.[7]

In this lecture, Renan is concerned to counter excessively determinist views of the nation and its history while accepting the power of historical ties. Against the ethnolinguistic criteria and militaristic nationalism of Heinrich von Treitschke and its use to justify German annexation of Alsace and Lorraine, the two provinces seized by Louis XIV, Renan observes that the nation is essentially a spiritual and political principle. It represents a fusion of races and remains a guarantee of liberty. It is largely the product of historical circumstances and to that extent contingent. At the same time, it is not a mere construct. European nations, he argues, can be traced back to the early Middle Ages: "It was, in fact, the Germanic invasions which introduced into the world the principle which, later, was to serve as a basis for the existence of nationalities" (Renan 1882, cited in Bhabha 1990, 9).

The partition of Verdun in 843 outlined divisions which were in principle immutable, and these became the basis for the subsequent nations of Western Europe. What the Germanic invaders brought was kingship, military aristocracies, and bounded (and named) territories, not race or language or culture. If conversion to Christianity and much linguistic forgetting helped to fuse populations, dynastic territories redivided them along political—that is, national—lines. Here we see the primary thrust of Renan's thesis. It is not a commitment to voluntary nationality, nor a belief in the individual's right to choose his or her nation. It is a vindication of the political definition of the nation and, secondarily, though in more muted vein, of the historic power of Germanic monarchical government.[8] But politics is not enough. The state as such cannot function as a social cement or a bond between its citizens. For Renan, that can be provided only by "history," or rather, by historical memories and the "cult of the ancestors."

"The nation, like the individual, is the culmination of a long past of endeavours, sacrifice and devotion. Of all cults, that of the ancestors is the most legitimate, for the ancestors have made us what we are. A heroic past, great men, glory (by which I understand genuine glory), this is the social capital upon which one bases a national idea. To have common glories in the past and to have a common will in the present; to have performed great deeds together, to wish to perform still more—these are the essential conditions for being a people" (Renan 1882, cited in Bhabha 1990, 19). For Renan, this means that shared suffering is more important than shared joy: "Where national memories are concerned, griefs are of more value than triumphs, for they impose duties, and require a common effort" (ibid.).

This brings Renan to his well-known definition: "A nation is therefore a large-scale solidarity, constituted by the feeling of the sacrifices one has made in the past and of those one is prepared to make in the future. It presupposes a past; it is summarised, however, in the present by a tangible fact, namely, consent, the clearly expressed desire to continue a common life. A nation's existence is, if you will pardon the metaphor, a daily plebiscite, just as the individual's existence is a perpetual affirmation of life" (ibid.).

In this often cited passage, the voluntarism that appears to inhere in the idea of a daily plebiscite is limited through a comparison with the perpetual affirmation of life by the individual; and just as, in practice, we are justified in assuming that most individuals will continue to make that affirmation, so we can equally assume that collective consent will not be witheld, that nations whose identities are based on shared memories will continue to affirm their common destinies. Nations may not be eternal, says Renan; "they had their beginnings and they will end." But neither are they ephemeral or optional. They are not mere communities of interest; in Renan's well-known words, "a *Zollverein* is not a *patrie.*" Man is certainly "a reasonable and moral being, before he is cooped up in such and such a language, before he is a member of such and such a race, before he belongs to such and such a culture. Before French, German, or Italian culture there is human culture" (Renan 1882, cited in Bhabha 1990, 17).

But at the same time, Renan insists that by the tenth century the power of linguistic forgetting had encouraged a situation in which "all the inhabitants of France are French," according to the first *chansons de geste*, and that the sharp difference between noble and serf in France "was in no sense presented as an ethnic difference." Hence, his ringing affirmation of the primacy of a universal human culture must be understood more as a normative statement, as the assertion of a moral ideal, than as a historical fact.

And here lies the crux of an abiding tension, not only in Renan's position, but in that of many scholars after him.[9] A similar tension between a Burkean adherence to national memory and tradition and a voluntaristic ideal of social contract can also be found in Lord Acton's denunciation of the Continental "unitary" doctrine of nationality. Here Acton contrasts two conceptions of nationality. In the English libertarian ideal, which harks back to the Glorious Revolution, the nation becomes "the bulwark of self-government, and the foremost limit to the excessive power of the State." In contrast, the French ideal, which is the source of Mazzini's political nationalism and the object of Acton's critique, takes its inspiration from the Revolution and "overrules the rights and wishes of the inhabitants, absorbing their divergent interests in a fictitious unity; sacrifices their several inclinations and duties to the higher claim of nationality, and crushes all natural rights and established liberties for the purpose of vindicating itself." For Acton, the Continental theory of nationality "is a retrograde step in history," and he concludes that "nationality does not aim either at liberty or prosperity, both of which it sacrifices to the imperative necessity of making the nation the mould and measure of the State. Its course will be marked with material as well as moral ruin, in order that a new invention may prevail over the works of God and the interests of mankind" (Acton 1948, 166–95).

For the conservative Catholic English historian, the unitary theory of nationality is seen as a political and a French invention, whereas for the French linguistic scholar, Renan, it was a German ethnographic theory of politics that had to be countered in the name of the apparently selfsame values of liberty and traditional authority. Shall we, then, need to distinguish a third conception of the nation—a Whig or English ideal of nationality based on the individual liberties espoused by Lord Acton—from both a French doctrine of the political will grounded on historic memories proclaimed by Renan and the German Romantic vision of organic ethnocultural nations, stemming from Herder and Fichte?

It is a question that we might address not only to Marx and Engels and their followers, but also to Max Weber.[10] As a German nationalist and historian, Weber appears to accept the Herderian vision of nations as *Stände*, cultural communities of prestige, when he writes that "the significance of the 'nation' is usually anchored in the superiority, or at least irreplaceability, of the cultural values that can only be preserved and developed through the cultivation of the individuality [*Eigenart*] of the community" (Weber 1968, 3:926).

At the same time, though he never completed his projected account of the rise of the nation-state in Europe, it is clear that Weber saw political action and political memories as the crucial forces that have shaped the evolution of modern nations. In this, he stands closer to French conceptions. Not only does Weber define the nation as a "community of sentiment which would adequately manifest itself in a state of its own," he returns more than once to the vexed problem of Alsace and Lorraine and the French sympathies and loyalties of their inhabitants. It is not language nor ethnicity nor geography that defines a people; in this he concurs with Renan. It is political history and, more specifically, political memories that determine national allegiances:

> The reason for the Alsatians not feeling themselves as belonging to the German nation has to be sought in their memories. Their political destiny has taken its course outside the German sphere for too long; for their heroes are the heroes of French history. If the custodian of the Colmar museum wants to show you which among his treasures he cherishes most, he takes you away from Grunwald's altar to a room filled with tricolors, *pompier*, and other helmets and souvenirs of a seemingly most insignificant nature; they are from a time that to him is a heroic age. (Weber 1947, 176)

And Weber explains this curious fact by recourse to political memory. Speaking of the Alsatians' attachment to tricolors, *pompier*, helmets, edicts by Louis Philippe, "and especially memorabilia from the French Revolution," Weber writes: "This sense of [French] community came into being by virtue of common political and, indirectly, social experiences which are highly valued by the masses as symbols of the destruction of feudalism, and the story of these events takes the place of the heroic legends of primitive peoples" (Weber 1968, 1:396).

Here it is not the Hegelian criterion of former statehood that marks out the historical nations but rather collective political memories of the kind emphasized by Renan. But, again like Renan, Weber places these memories in the context of cultural and political nations able to point to memorable ethnic pasts. While both Renan and Weber resist organic definitions of nationality for conceptions based on political memories and collective will, they do so against the background of a pervasive Romantic belief in the longevity and power of historic nations. (See Beetham 1974; Guibernau 1996, chap. 1.)

Ethnic and Civic Nations

What relevance, we may ask, have these essentially nineteenth-century debates for the utterly changed circumstances of the end of the twentieth century? Do they possess anything more than a purely antiquarian interest? Certainly, in the aftermath of the horrors of the Second World War, these debates of earlier historians about nations suddenly came to appear esoteric and passé. Who could possibly embrace any version of nationalism, let alone an organic conception of the nation? Was this not the poisoned seedbed of fascism and Nazism? In John Dunn's doom-laden words: "Nationalism is the starkest political shame of the twentieth century, the deepest, most intractable and yet most unanticipated blot on the political history of the world since the year 1900" (Dunn 1978, 55). Yet even as he wrote, the ethnic revival of peripheral neonationalisms in the West had been in full swing for a decade and was soon to be joined by a dramatic resurgence of ethnic nationalisms in Eastern Europe and the former Soviet Union. The result has been not only a popular rush to "rediscover" nationalism in place of an obsolescent communism but a renewed, if wary, scholarly interest in the subject of nationalism and even in the ethnic conception of the nation. What could such a conceptual revolution signify?

At the popular level, a revitalized ethnic nationalism could imply a disturbing historical amnesia or a desire to disentangle the ethnic nation from the entrapments of a *volkish* racism while retaining its popular base. On the other hand, it might be a response to the ubiquitous stranger and, in Eric Hobsbawm's words, to our sense of "fragility, or the drying up of our own family roots," as well as marking profound disappointment at the failure of more universal visions like socialism. Alternatively, we might, with Ernest Gellner, see this headlong return to ethnic nationalism as a necessary reentry of peoples and nations into the relevant time zone of modernity, once the nightmares of

Nazism and communism had passed (Hobsbawm 1990, 164, 167, 178; Gellner 1994, 23–31).[11]

The scholarly return to nationalism is, of course, much more circumspect. The ethnic version remains profoundly suspect. It is widely equated with the exclusiveness of "blood" associated with the organic version of nationalism. Thus, Michael Ignatieff distinguishes a benign "civic" form of nationalism from an aggressive and exclusive "ethnic" version—the kind that fertilized and fueled the recent wars between Serbs and Croats in Bosnia. Similarly, the social philosopher David Miller, for all his criticism of the inadequacy of Habermas's ideal of "constitutional patriotism," tends to prefer a civic ideal of nationalism that resembles Renan's political voluntarism. Critical of the claims of ethnic separatists, Miller strips his definition of nationality of any ethnic characteristics, referring only to public culture (Ignatieff 1993 and 1998, chap. 2; Miller 1995, chap. 1).[12]

Sociologists, too, have found the distinction between ethnic and civic nationalisms useful. Raymond Breton traces the evolution of both English Canada and, to a lesser extent, Quebec from an exclusive ethnic nationalism based on White British or French Catholic culture to an inclusive multicultural civic nationalism welcoming large numbers of non-White immigrants and celebrating a diversity of cultures. In Australia, Stephen Castles and his associates have pointed to a similar trajectory from a conservative White British ethnic nationalism to a more open, civic, and multicultural Australian identity that from the 1960s has welcomed large-scale Asian immigration, if not so readily the aboriginal inhabitants. (See Castles et al. 1988; Breton 1988.)

These essentially normative and sociological accounts have their counterparts in historical analyses. Already, in Elie Kedourie's forthright diatribe against nationalism, we meet the familiar Actonian dichotomy of an acceptable Whig doctrine of nationality and a pernicious Continental theory of unitary nationalism. However, the object of Kedourie's polemic is no longer the Rousseauian and Mazzinian doctrine of political will but Fichte's political synthesis of Kant's doctrine of self-determination and Herder's ideal of cultural and linguistic diversity. For Kedourie, this baleful German Romantic doctrine of nationalism must be attributed to the social and political exclusion of alienated and restless German intellectuals, but even more to the intellectual and moral arrogance of the Enlightenment quest for terrestrial perfectibility. We can go further: the progressive radicalism of the Enlightenment can in turn be traced back to the heterodox doctrines of a medieval Christian millennialism, with its wild apocalyptic expectation of an imminent Second Coming, so like nationalism in its antinomian subversion of public order and established authority (Kedourie 1960 and 1971, introduction).

A similar doctrinal distinction but without the chiliastic roots can be found in Maurizio Viroli's *For Love of Country* (1995). Viroli's account opposes two political traditions: a much older civic tradition, grounded in the Roman political legacy of republican liberty, and a much more recent ethnocultural ideal, based on German Romantic conceptions of the nation stemming from Herder and Fichte. Viroli too is dissatisfied with Habermas's cosmopolitan "constitutional patriotism"; it is too abstract, too removed from real liberty and a well-ordered society. In contrast, the republican patriotism that he espouses is territorially particularist: it is grounded in distinct political institutions, definite territories, and real histories, and it seeks to link individual and collective freedom to a history of civic heroism and pride. Ethnocultural nationalism, on the other hand, subordinates individual and collective liberties to the demand for cultural homogeneity and national unity. It is not concerned with the liberties and prosperity of the citizens in a well-ordered, law-abiding republic, nor does it engender a caring compassion for fellow-citizens. Nationalism's overriding concern with unity and homogeneity inevitably breeds an exclusive and narrow love of the nation.

As a contribution to the classical civic and libertarian tradition, this account is not without its attractions. But it is also fundamentally flawed. For one thing, it is lacking in sociological realism. The republican virtues may be well suited to the city-state formations from which they sprang, but they will hardly suffice for large, populous, and often varied nations. In these circumstances a nationalism that stresses cultural unity, if not homogeneity, is required to instil the necessary solidarity and purpose in an often heterogeneous society. That, surely, is one of the reasons for the triumph of nationalism, whose success Viroli bemoans. Besides, Viroli fails to see that his vision of republican liberty, when applied to a larger canvas, is really only a variant of the more general civic form of nationalism, and as such it is quite as closely aligned with the ideals of Rousseau and Renan as with those of the Italian theorists he discusses. He also exaggerates the differences between the civic republican doctrine and the more populist cultural vision of Herder and Fichte. As his own example of Mazzini's fusion of these ideologies shows, the distinction is of only limited empirical use. Mazzini's belief that civic liberty could flourish only in a culturally unified nation demonstrates, once again, that, however useful the distinction between civic and cultural forms of nationalism may be as an analytic tool, it has serious empirical limitations. The moment we ask who are the people who are entitled to enjoy the liberties and prosperity of citizenship in a well-ordered *national* society, we are forced back onto some cultural criterion of boundedness, however loose. The result, in so many historical cases, is that the civic-territorial and ethnocultural ideals of the nation are closely interwoven; thinkers, movements, periods may oscillate between them, or they may be run together without much regard for logical consistency. The dramatic history of nineteenth-century French nationalisms illustrates the ambiguities, tensions, and inconsistencies of the uses to which these conceptions can be and have been put. At times they may run in tandem; at other times they may come into conflict, most notably during the Dreyfus Affair (Kedward 1965; Gildea 1994).[13]

Nor can we claim that civic and political forms of nationalism are necessarily more open and tolerant than ethnocultural forms. Despite their fraternal rhetoric, they are capable of imposing an uniformity every bit as draconian and exclusive as those nationalisms that espouse genealogical criteria of membership. It is true, as Rogers Brubaker has shown, that German citizenship laws invoking *ius sanguinis* are in theory more exclusive than their French counterparts, based as the latter are on *ius soli*. In this respect it is common to contrast the German refusal till very recently to consider naturalizing immigrants and *Gastarbeiter*, while according automatic citizenship to ethnic Germans from the East, with the French policy of assimilating colonial and ex-colonial African and Asian immigrants, or at least some of them, into French culture. But citizenship law is only one part of the national ensemble and perhaps not the most decisive. Social and cultural acceptance of foreigners is as elusive in France as it is in Germany, and right-wing xenophobia and demagoguery is as rife west of the Rhine and Rhône as it is to the east (Brubaker 1992; Miles 1993).

Moreover, the price of integration can be just as high under civic forms of nationalism. Minorities, like the Jews who sought French citizenship or were summoned to seek entry into French society, had to pay a high price for acceptance: the surrender of their ethnic particularity and their collective rights and culture. "To the Jews as a nation we give nothing, to the Jews as individuals we give everything," declared Clermont-Tonnerre in 1790, and it fell to Napoleon to carry through that principle to its logical conclusion. Not that admission to the French polity greatly helped the Jews of France. They were soon attacked from the Left as well as the Right, in the name of equality as much as of tradition. Equality proved to be a very French ideal; it was open only to *French* citizens—those who could show that they were truly French by embracing French culture, language, and history with all their being and forswearing any other history and cultural identity. That this culture had been forged under the auspices of Catholicism and that it was underpinned by the history of a Christian kingdom—for all that religion and monarchy might now be rejected and displaced—remained a constant, if hidden, foundation of the cultural edifice called "modern France"; and this was not lost on ethnic minorities of a different (and suspect) religious faith, such as the Jews. (See Vital 1975, 25; Schwarzfuchs 1979.)[14]

It might be objected that French, like Catalan, nationalism is not a species of civic but of "cultural" or linguistic nationalism, a form to be distinguished from the genealogical basis of ethnic nationalism and the territorial referent of civic nationalism and one that requires of outsiders only full socialization into the host language and culture to gain social acceptance. Once again, in logic there may be a good case for such a distinction, but in practice it is difficult to find any examples of a "pure" cultural nationalism, freed from its ethnic moorings. It is certainly not to be found in Europe. Even in the United States, even leaving aside the Blacks and Native Americans, ethnic origin remained an important, even crucial criterion of acceptance until well into the 1960s and perhaps beyond, as it remains in Britain and France to this day (Glazer and Moynihan 1975, introduction; Conversi 1998).

What such a distinction assumes is a secular trend from ethnic toward civic nationalism, with cultural nationalism as a kind of halfway house along the road. But the evidence for such a trend, even in the West, is dubious. Italians are not prepared to accept

Albanian refugees even if they can show that they are willing to be socialized into the Italian language and culture, nor are the French ready to accord such cultural acceptance to North African Muslims. German attitudes to Turks and Vietnamese; Czech attitudes to Gypsies; Swiss to Italian *Gastarbeiter*; Basque to Andalusian immigrants do not suggest any diminution of exclusive boundaries or ethnic consciousness, even in advanced industrial societies. Even the Scottish quotation from the Reverend McIntosh that we saw on flagpole banners in Stirling in 1997 on the seven-hundredth anniversary of William Wallace's victory over the English at Stirling Bridge, which read: "Nothing makes me more proud of my nation than to hear a foreigner—whether Polish, Pakistani, Chinese or English—begin to speak with a touch of the local accent; to hear the solid dialect of the hills and the streets grow in their conversation; to feel their exile lighten a little as they become infected with that unsentimental and instinctive love that finds its happiest expression in what passes between us, and which is the only true patriotism," even such an apparently purely cultural patriotism presupposes a *myth* of Scottish ancestral origins and shared historical memories of the homeland that defines the ethnic basis of a supposedly entirely civic Scottish nation.[15]

All this, of course, is far removed from the biological (and even racial) assumptions that underlay the organic analogy and that sometimes, though by no means always, permeated the earlier organic kind of nationalism. Ethnicity here is more a matter of cultural than biological origins and growth. Nevertheless, given this vital qualification, in the confusion of the post–cold war world we are witnessing as many movements toward ethnic nationalism, notably in Eastern Europe and the former Soviet Union but also in the West (not to mention Asia and Africa), as there are trends toward more civic forms of nationalisms; and in most cases civic elements are mingled, in varying proportions, with ethnic components.

Cultural Primordialism

Should we then infer that ethnic attachments are indispensable to nations and nationalisms, as the organic historicists assumed?

That, certainly, is what the foregoing analysis would appear to suggest. In the same way that we saw the first nationalists and early historians of nationalism seeking to combine and reflect on the permutations of these various elements, so too today we need to set aside simplistic distinctions and evolutionary trends to uncover the deeper sources of popular attachments to collective cultural identities.

This is where the so-called cultural primordialists have made an important, if misunderstood, contribution. They point to the continuing force of ethnic attachments, which often undergird the contractual rights and duties of a modern civic order. Communities of language, myths of origin, shared memories and customs, and attachments to homelands are just some of the enduring cultural attributes that (in the tradition of Durkheim) Edward Shils (1957) and Clifford Geertz (1973) sought to highlight when they distinguished primordial from civil ties in modern societies—whether in respect of rituals like the British coronation ceremony or of ethnic attachments in the new states of Africa and Asia.

For Geertz, ethnic and national attachments spring from the "cultural givens" of social existence—from contiguity and kinship, language, religion, race, and customs. He went on to claim that many peoples' "sense of self is bound up in the gross actualities of blood, race, language, locality, religion or tradition." But he then introduced a vital qualification: "By a primordial attachment is meant one that stems from the 'givens'—or more precisely, as culture is inevitably involved in such matters, the assumed 'givens' of social existence. . . . These congruities of blood, speech, custom, and so on, are seen to have an ineffable, and at times, overpowering, coerciveness in and of themselves" (Geertz 1973, 259–60).

In other words, primordial attachments rest on perception, cognition, and belief. It is individual members who assume that these cultural features are givens, who attribute overwhelming importance to these ties, who feel an overpowering sense of coerciveness, and so on. They possess a power beyond rational calculation and interest—because people attribute that power and meaning to them, not because of the nature of the primordial tie in itself. These, then, are the subjective sources of collective cultural identities, and they should form the main object of analysis for historians and social scientists of ethnicity and nationalism. That was how Geertz himself sought to approach the politics of the new states of Africa and Asia. The drive to create and live in an efficient, orderly state and civil society simply served to exacerbate these primordial attachments, because the sovereign state introduced a new prize for rival ethnic communities over which to fight and a frightening new force with which to contend (Geertz 1973, 270).[16]

How can such a broad anthropological understanding aid the historical analysis of ethnicity and nationalism? And what are the limitations of this approach for a historiography of nations and nationalism? This was the subject of an interesting debate between Paul Brass and Francis Robinson on the historical factors involved in the formation of Pakistan. Brass had argued that the Muslim elites had mobilized the Muslim masses by manipulating Islamic symbols, to preserve their own economic and political position at a time when British rule in India seemed to turn against their interests in favor of the Hindu elites that dominated the Indian Congress Party. Brass was critical of the failure of primordialist models to deal with historical change and to address the variability of religious, linguistic, and ethnic attachments or predict the rise of nationalism. He therefore opted for a more instrumentalist framework, which saw Muslim ethnicity in India and the rise of Pakistani nationalism as products of elite manipulation of existing symbolic resources (Brass 1979, 35–77).

For Robinson, on the other hand, Muslim attachments and the ideology of the *umma* played a crucial role in persuading Muslim elites of the need to safeguard their distinctive heritage and community by seeking greater autonomy and ultimately independence for the Muslims concentrated in the United Provinces in the northwest and in Bengal. For Robinson, the growth of Muslim sentiment, the presence of collective historical memories and the centrality of the tradition of the *umma*, meant that "Islamic ideas and values . . . both provide a large part of the framework of norms and desirable ends within which the United Provinces Muslim elite take their rational political decisions, and on occasion act as a motivating force" (Robinson 1979, 78–82). In other words, preexisting, premodern religious attachments and historical memories were crucial in constraining the Muslim elites and molding their outlooks and actions.

Once again, it is important not to overstate the differences between these two positions. Robinson is quite ready to analyze the political rationality of Muslim elite actions in creating a Pakistani state for a Muslim ethnic community; primordial attachments are not nonrational, let alone irrational. On his side, Brass concedes the importance of cultural traditions in molding elite outlooks and actions, as well as in providing the symbolic resources necessary for mobilizing the Muslim masses in India. Indeed, where an ethnic group can draw on an old and rich cultural heritage with a persisting core, such as the Jews can with their talmudic traditions, and where this cultural heritage is reinforced by a strong institutional framework like the rabbinate, Brass regards the impact of cultural attachments as particularly powerful and lasting (Brass 1991, chap. 2).

Nevertheless, the primordialist contribution is significant in stressing exactly those dimensions of subjective emotion and intimate belonging that the cultural nationalists had singled out and that political, economic, and military history failed to address. Herder himself put the point succinctly. Speaking of the importance of literature for a nation, he asked:

Has a nation anything more precious? From a study of native literature we have learned to know ages and peoples more deeply than along the sad and frustrating path of political and military history. In the latter we seldom see more than the manner in which a people was ruled, how it let itself be slaughtered; in the former we learn how it thought, what it wished and craved for, how it took its chief pleasures, how it was led by its teachers and its inclinations. (Herder [1877–1913], 18: 137; cited in Berlin 1976, 169)

More deeply: that is the plea of the sociolinguistic historian Joshua Fishman (1980), when he argues that, to grasp the meaning and force of ethnicity, we must set aside the liberal, radical, and sociological assumptions of modernism. Ethnicity is perennial, if not primordial. It was felt and articulated among ancient Greeks and Hebrews, as well as in the early Church and the Eastern branches of Christianity; and after the transformations wrought by mercantilism and industrialization in Europe, its claims were forcibly restated by Herder and his followers.[17] For Fishman, ethnicity is a matter of "being," "doing," and "knowing." As a phenomenon of being, "ethnicity has always been experienced as a kinship phenomenon, a continuity within the self and within those who share an intergenerational link to common ancestors. Ethnicity is partly experienced as being 'bone of their bone, flesh of their flesh, and blood of their blood'" (84–85).

But unmobilized ethnicity is not simply a matter of kinship and biology nor of ethnic "being." It also involves "doing" and "knowing." It demands from members authentic activities and behavior that seek to preserve and augment the heritage of ancestors, and it requires genuine ethnic responses and wisdom, preferably in an authentic linguistic medium. This means that ethnicity is never fixed. It is always adaptable and forward-looking; its only requirement is that new things should be done "in our own way" and that we remain "true to our genius." This is exactly what the historical record of ethnicity and ethnic nationalism in Eastern Europe demonstrates.

Of course, there are many problems with this kind of analysis. For one thing, it is not clear how we can verify the collective sentiments of the majority of the people of an *ethnie*, especially in premodern periods. For another, for all his claims about ethnic adaptability, there is a curiously static feeling about Fishman's (1980) depiction of the immemorial persistence of ethnicity as "a tangible, living reality that makes every human a link in an eternal bond from generation to generation," particularly when we think of the modern world with its mass migrations, refugees, colonization, genocide, large-scale intermarriage, bilingualism, and mixed heritages (85). Nor is it easy to see how one might apply Fishman's general approach to specific historical sequences of events; it appears to offer no explanatory model to account for particular ethnic communities and identities—their emergence, character, vicissitudes, and decline. But perhaps most crucially for our purposes, Joshua Fishman fails to address the question of the relationship between a perennial ethnicity, on the one hand, and nations and nationalism, on the other hand; indeed, he seems to think it is all one thing. But with so much evidence pointing the other way, such a sweeping transhistorical standpoint must be fully argued rather than simply assumed.

These weaknesses stem, I think, from the primordial elements in Fishman's approach. For, although he does not share the more theoretical primordia*list* interests of Geertz and his followers, Fishman is equally persuaded of the power, ubiquity, and durability of ethnic attachments throughout history. Fishman is right to stress this "participants' primordialism"—that is to say, the members' sense of the immemorial nature of their own ethnic ties—which is, indeed, a vital element of the *explanandum*. These vivid attachments, their power and longevity, are exactly what must be explained. But as a transhistorical paradigm that derives ethnicity and nationhood from the ties of kinship and territory, cultural primordialism is unable to provide a convincing historical account of ethnic or national phenomena. It can offer only a very general and rather speculative thesis about the continuing role of the cultural givens—kinship and territory, language and religion—but it is a thesis that of its nature can never amount to a causal historical explanation.[18]

Conclusion

Nevertheless, with all its limitations, cultural primordialism is important for two reasons. Theoretically, it exposes the weaknesses of instrumentalist historical accounts: their exaggerated belief in the powers of elite manipulation of the masses; their failure to take seriously the symbolic aspects of nationalism; their ethnocentric bias, with the West as the norm and pressure group politics as the model; and their blindness to the roles of both the sacred and ethnicity in kindling mass fervor and self-sacrifice.

At the empirical level, too, cultural primordialism exposes the failure of purely voluntaristic and interest-based explanations to see how ethnic and cultural dimensions have been present even in the most secular and rationalist kinds of nationalism. It is exactly the so-called organic and primordial features of nations and nationalisms, which Rousseau, Herder, and the Romantics first highlighted, that we need to recall: the role of "sacred ethnicity" in the rituals and ideals of the French Revolution and the elements of pan-Turkist historicism in secular Turkish nationalism, of Russian national fervor in Stalin's Soviet Union, of mystical naturalism in early socialist Zionism and liberal Indian nationalism—to take some of the more secular, civic, and modernizing examples. In other words, each nationalism and every concept of the nation is composed of different elements and dimensions, which we choose to label voluntarist and organic, civic and ethnic, primordial and instrumental. No nation, no nationalism, can be seen as purely the one or the other, even if at certain moments one or other of these elements predominates in the ensemble of components of national identity.

It is this plurality of components that we need to recognize as an inevitable part of the political world we inhabit. To attempt to excise one or other of these components from the received sense of popular national identity—the agenda of some political philosophers today—is unlikely to produce a world of mutually recognized and satisfied nations. To do so is to deny one of the central realities of the modern world: a world of complex nations, powered by nationalisms that have fused the drive for popular sovereignty and participation with the widespread desire for intimate belonging in a historic culture community. In my view, humanizing and balancing these desires is preferable to trying to abolish the one in favor of the other or to denying both in the name of some abstract cosmopolitan ideal.

2   The Nation

Modern or Perennial?

The first question in this inquiry concerned the character of nations and nationalism. The second focuses on their historical location and embeddedness. This raises the complex problem of periodization: to which period in history, if any, nations and nationalism may be said properly to belong. This has become, in many ways, the central issue in the study of nations and nationalism and the ground of what Adrian Hastings has called "our historiographical schism." As we shall see, it also furnishes the basis of a major political and sociological divide.

The Modernist Orthodoxy

In the past, many scholars and most of the educated public assumed that nations and nationalism were, if not primordial, at least perennial. Nations could be found everywhere in the historical record, even if they were not part of nature or the human condition per se. These scholars might concede that nationa*lism*, the deliberate movement to awaken nations, was fairly recent; but the nation itself was immemorial, coeval with recorded history, even if individual nations slumbered and had to be "awoken" to their ancient destiny. (See Walek-Czernecki 1929; Pearson 1993).[1]

The Second World War shattered these half-conscious assumptions. Even if many members of the educated public still cling to the belief that the roots of their own nations can be traced back for several centuries, most scholars today have abandoned the old *perennialism*. Instead, today's dominant orthodoxy is thoroughly *modernist*. Modernists contend that

1. national*ist* ideologies, as well as the system of nation-states, are modern, that is, both recent in date and novel in character;

2. nations and national identities are also recent and novel;
3. and most important, nations and nationalisms are the product of modernization and modernity.

The first of these propositions has won almost universal acceptance. Scholars generally date the beginnings of the European system of nation-states to the Treaty of Westphalia in 1648, from whence it spread to other parts of the world, mainly through colonialism (Tilly 1975, introduction and conclusion). As for nationalist ideologies, interwar pioneers of the study of nationalism—Carlton Hayes, Louis Snyder, and Hans Kohn, as well as Edward Carr and Alfred Cobban slightly later—documented the emergence of its varieties from the eighteenth century in what we might call a sober historical manner, that is, without any special ideological or sociological bias. (See Hayes 1931; Kohn [1944] 1967a; Carr 1945; Cobban [1945] 1969.)[2]

It is the second proposition that has attracted much greater debate. The thesis that nations are both recent and novel was championed by Kohn, Carr, and Cobban, as well as by the Marxists; but it was disputed, in varying degrees, by Johan Huizinga, Marc Bloch, Joseph Strayer, and George Coulton, who argued for a late medieval dating for the emergence of nations and national sentiment. Others, like Frederick Hertz, Ernst Kantorowicz, and Boyd Shafer, adopted a compromise position, pointing to the strength of medieval national sentiments while agreeing that these differed in vital respects from modern nationalisms. (See Hertz 1944; Shafer 1955; Bloch 1961, 2:432–37; Davis 1967.)[3]

But the most contentious of the propositions is undoubtedly the last. And its adoption marks out "true" modernism. Nations, it claims, have a "modern" character because they are the product of the novel conditions and spirit of "modernity"; they could appear only when these novel conditions and the spirit of modernity had begun to act like a solvent on traditional societies. We might call this position sociological, as opposed to purely chronological, modernism (A. D. Smith 1998, chap. 1).

This was the central point made, in their different ways, by both Elie Kedourie and Ernest Gellner. Kedourie was concerned to derive nationalist ideologies from the peculiar *zeitgeist* of the Enlightenment and Romanticism. He traced their philosophical lineage back to the Cartesian quest for certainty and the Enlightenment belief in the mastery of reason and the necessity of progress. Specifically, he credited Immanuel Kant with fathering the ideal of the struggle for self-determination of the national will, although Kant himself predicated his ethics on the individual quest for autonomy of the good will. It was Johann Gottlieb Fichte and his followers who attached this quest to national communities, which they identified with Herder's ideal of cultural diversity through the realization of pure national language groups. Socially, too, Kedourie located the origins of nationalist ideology among the restless youth and alienated intellectuals excluded from power in the German principalities and, much later, among the same class of rejected "marginal men" in colonial Africa and Asia. In short, for Kedourie, nationalism is recent, novel, European, and invented—and as such profoundly subversive of political and social order. It is an act of will, an unattainable dream of perfectibility on earth to be achieved through untold violence and suffering; and in these respects it resembles and derives from the antinomian medieval Christian millennial movements so vividly described by Norman Cohn, although its modern manifestations are secular and revolutionary (Kedourie 1960 and 1971, introduction; Cohn 1957).[4]

To Kedourie's historical account, Ernest Gellner added a broad sociological analysis. He too argued that nations and nationalism are modern, that is, both recent and novel. There could be no room for nations in premodern, agroliterate societies, because the tiny elites in such societies were totally isolated from the great mass of food producers who were themselves divided into vertical folk cultures. As for the elites, they had no interest in spreading their culture to the masses; the only elite that might have wanted to do so, the clergy, lacked the means. So nationalism is an entirely modern phenomenon. It is also functional and necessary for industrialism, because an industrial society requires a "high culture" to operate and succeed, one that is specialist, literate, and based on mass, standardized schooling.

How did this profound change come about? For Gellner, the tidal wave of modernization eroded traditional role-based societies and replaced them with literate "high" cultures in the swollen, anonymous urban centers. Today we are all "clerks," and literacy through a standardized, public education is the passport to citizenship. But the tidal wave of modernization is also uneven: it creates conflicts between the old city inhabitants and the newly uprooted peasants-turned-workers. If the newcomers look different, speak a different language, or have a different textual religion, social conflicts turn into ethnic antagonisms; and this encourages the newcomers to secede and set up their own cultural nation. Thus, beneath its fanciful romanticism, nationalism is an objective, practical necessity; and it is nationalism that invents nations where they do not exist, even if it needs some preexisting cultural markers to aid the process of nation creation. Modernity is therefore always nationalist, and though it may be logically contingent, nationalism is sociologically necessary in the modern world (Gellner 1964, chap. 7, and 1983).[5]

Modernist Historiography

Though many historians had already accepted a chronological modernism, it is only since the 1960s, following Karl Deutsch, Kedourie, and Gellner, that many historians have also embraced a sociological modernism and have sought to demonstrate how the advent of modernity was alone able to create a world of nations and nation-states, along with nationalist ideologies. Indeed, for many of these historians, it is the modern professionalized state, powered by capitalism and industrialism, that has been responsible for the rise and spread of nations and nationalism. (See Deutsch 1966; Tilly 1975, introduction and conclusion; Kamenka 1976; Tivey 1980; Alter 1989.)

Let me illustrate this proposition with two examples. The first is John Breuilly's view that nationalism is a strictly modern and a purely political movement. Its aim, he claims, is to capture and retain state power, and it does so by advancing nationalist arguments. These he defines as follows:

A nationalist argument is a political doctrine built on three assertions:
(a) There exists a nation with an explicit and peculiar character.
(b) The interests and values of this nation take priority over all other interests and values.
(c) The nation must be as independent as possible. This usually requires the attainment of at least political sovereignty. (Breuilly 1993, 2)[6]

These arguments appeal to various sub-elites, whom the nationalist leaders mobilize and coordinate and whose project of capturing and retaining state power they legitimate. But they possess this appeal only under certain conditions: when capitalist modernization has separated the absolutist state from civil society and created a gulf between the two. This situation leaves many educated people with a sense of frustration and alienation, and they turn to doctrines that promise a reintegration of the modern state with society. That is why the historicist arguments advanced by Herder exert such an appeal. Herder's historicism appeared to reintegrate state and society by calling on the members of a community to restore it to its natural, authentic state. But this can be achieved only by realizing its true self and redefining the cultural nation as the political nation. For Breuilly, such a sleight-of-hand redefinition is spurious; yet he concedes that nationalism was trying to make a serious, if mistaken, attempt to address a real problem (ibid., 55–64).

Breuilly tends to regard nationalist ideology as secondary to the political contexts and aims of the movement. Nevertheless, in his vivid analysis of the myths and symbols of Afrikaner nationalism, he illustrates the hold of nationalist ideologies and concedes their superior appeal to other ideologies. He points to the powerful message of the Great Trek and the Day of the Covenant when a small force of Boer farmers defeated the large Zulu armies at the Battle of Blood River in 1838. Yet it was only much later, in Kruger's republic, that the Day of the Covenant was instituted; and it was only a century later, in the great Ossawatrek of 1938, that the myth helped to ensure a measure of Afrikaner political unity.[7] It did so, as do all nationalisms, through its strong self-referential and salvation symbolism: "Nationalists celebrate themselves rather than some transcendent reality" (ibid., 64); "The central message, conveyed through anthems, rallies, speeches and elaborate ceremonials, is of an embattled people. The aim is to return to the heights of the past, though in a transformed fashion" (ibid., 67–68).

However, this insight into the power of myth and ceremonial is absent in Breuilly's brief analysis of the rise of the first German nation-state in the period 1800 to 1871. Here again he gives pride of place to politics and the state, especially the political, military, and economic competition between Prussia and Austria. Cultural factors are not neglected, but there is little reference to Romantic ideologies and movements and none to earlier popular myths, memories, and symbols of Germania, which flourished among the German humanists in the Renaissance and were revived in the eighteenth century. It is power politics, not ideology or cultural identity, that created the first German "nation-state" (Breuilly 1996b, chap. 2; cf. Barnard 1965; Berlin 1976, 147–51).[8]

And in *that* sense, Breuilly is right. But the creation of the German "nation-state"—itself an ambiguous and contested concept—is only part of the story. It is not the same as the creation of a German "nation." To explain why a *German* nation succeeded over possible rivals requires us to consider a different range of factors—social, cultural, and psychological. Why was it that Germania triumphed over Prussia (or even Austria)? Why did the secondary ideologies of the weak stratum of intellectuals prove victorious? If the boundaries of a Prussian-dominated *Kleindeutschland* were set by Bismarck's realpolitik, why were so many more German-speaking people ready to rally to the call of Germany and define those borders as those of a *German* homeland, a home to ethnic and linguistic Germans? (See Mosse 1976; Llobera 1994.)

My second example is an equally forthright modernist in both the chronological and sociological senses. For all his Marxism, Eric Hobsbawm (1990) is equally insistent on the political aspects of nationalism: its state-building propensity and the primacy of politics over culture. Nations are the products of nationalists whose goal is the creation of independent territorial states: "Nations only exist as functions of a particular kind of territorial state or the aspiration to establish one—broadly speaking, the citizen state of the French Revolution—but also in the context of a particular stage of technological and economic development" (9–10).

Hobsbawm goes on to show how the original version of nationalism that flourished in Europe from 1830 to 1870 was a democratic and political movement to establish the inclusive civic nation of the French Revolution and, as such, presupposed a large territory and large-scale market economy. After 1870, right up to 1914, this civic national ideal was challenged by a much more divisive kind of nationalism, based on ethnic and linguistic criteria and applicable in principle to any group of people that asserted its right to constitute an "unhistorical" nation. Here Hobsbawm echoes Hegel's theory of "historyless peoples," and like Engels, he reserves his greatest contempt for the many small-scale, fissiparous, ethnolinguistic nationalisms of Central and Eastern Europe. He bemoans the apparent resurgence of this divisive kind of nationalism since 1989 but regards it as a secondary and complicating factor, no longer a "major vector" of historical change in a globalizing era (Hobsbawm 1990, chaps. 4, 6).[9]

This insistence on the primacy of politics and the modern state sits strangely with Hobsbawm's Marxism. This is not so much because of the relegation of the economic factor to the background as of the primacy accorded to government and elites. What of the popular basis of nationalism? Is this simply another massive case of false consciousness and bourgeois manipulation? In his chapter on popular communities and bonds, Hobsbawm sidesteps this problem by claiming that the masses did indeed possess their own social and cultural traditions of community—regional, religious, or linguistic—but that these "proto-national" bonds are irrelevant to the subsequent modern political movement of nationalism. They cannot be regarded in any sense as ancestors or progenitors of nationalism "because they had or have no *necessary* relation with the unit of territorial political organisation which is a crucial criterion of what we understand as a 'nation' today" (ibid., 47, italics in original).

Note the extreme modernism of "we understand" and the reference to a nation "today" in this passage, as well as the extrusion of all reference to culture and identity in the criteria of modern nationhood. The exceptions that Hobsbawm admits to this generalization are interesting. They include England and France, Serbia and Russia, all of which retained memories of having belonged to a lasting political community, usually a medieval kingdom, land, and church, like Holy Russia. But they exclude the Germans and the Jews—the former because there could be no connection between modern German nationalism and medieval German ethnolinguistic and political ties; the latter because, since the Babylonian Captivity, Jews seem never to have desired a Jewish political, let alone territorial, state until the advent of Zionism. Hobsbawm continues: "It is entirely illegitimate to identify the Jewish links with the ancestral land of Israel, the merit deriving from pilgrimages there, or the hope of return there when the Messiah came—as he so obviously had *not* come in the view of the Jews—with the desire to gather all Jews into a modern territorial state situated on the ancient Holy Land" (ibid., 47–48, italics in original).

Like Breuilly, Hobsbawm dismisses the powerful myths, symbols, and memories of Germania held by the German Renaissance humanists and revived in the age of Klopstock, Novalis, Lessing, and Herder that became the basis for the activities of the German nationalist movement directed against Napoleon and later against Metternich's settlement. As for the Jews, leaving aside such matters as the Hasmonean state, the Zealots and Bar-Kochba's revolt, Hobsbawm shares with Gellner the idea that Israel is a wholly modern *nation* (not just a modern *state*) faced with purely modern challenges and problems. But such a view is hardly tenable, as it so obviously omits the raison d'être of the modern Jewish nation and state—its name, its location, its language, its Law of Return, its memories, symbols, values, myths, and traditions. (See Mosse 1976; Mendels 1992; Breuilly 1996b; Shimoni 1995.)[10]

The Perennialist Critique

In recent years, modernist historiography has come under attack from those historians who regard at least some of today's nations and even their nationalisms as premodern and even perennial. It also has been attacked by scholars who view the nation as a transhistorical phenomenon, recurring in many periods and continents, irrespective of economic, political, or cultural conditions.

In this "neo-perennialist" camp we can distinguish two tendencies. The first we may call *continuous perennialism*. It sees the roots of present-day nations extending back several centuries, in a few cases even millennia, into the distant past. This is the reality behind the perception of so many members that their nation is immemorial and perennial. This group of scholars tend to stress *continuity*. While acknowledging breaks and ruptures in the historical record, they point to the cultural continuities and identities over long time spans, which bind medieval or even ancient nations to their more recent counterparts. In these respects, modernization and modernity have been, if not irrelevant, certainly of lesser significance to the origins and development of nations and nationalism.

The second tendency can be termed *recurrent perennialism*. A few recent scholars regard the nation-in-general as a category of human association that can be found everywhere throughout history. As a result, they stress *recurrence* of an identical phenomenon. Particular nations, national identities and even nationalisms may come and go, but the phenomenon itself is universal and, as a form of association and collective identity, disembedded. As one might expect, the boundaries between these two tendencies of perennialism are not rigid. But those who emphasize national continuity tend to be medieval historians, whereas those who stress recurrence are either social scientists or ancient historians. But both tendencies attack modernist historiography, which is generally the preserve of modern historians, for its historical shallowness; its narrowly modernist definitions of the nation and nationalism; its preoccupation with citizenship, capitalism, and other facets of modernization; and frequently for an excessive instrumentalism that fails to give due weight to subjective factors.

Continuous Perennialism

In the postwar period, Hugh Seton-Watson stood out for refusing to accept a fully modernist position. While conceding that national*ism*, the ideology and movement, was both recent and novel, he drew a distinction between what he called the "old, continuous nations" and the much more recent nations created deliberately by national*ism*, especially in Eastern Europe and Asia.[11] (These latter are what Charles Tilly called "nations of design.") Such deliberately and often swiftly created nations, usually the outcome of treaties consequent upon periods of protracted warfare, like the Napoleonic wars or the First World War, include such nations as the Czechs and Slovaks, Rumanians, Bulgarians, Serbs and Croats, Ukrainians, Estonians, Azeris, Kurds, Syrians, Pakistanis, Malaysians, and Indonesians. The "old, continuous nations" could trace their origins back to the Middle Ages; they include France, England, Scotland, Holland, Castile, Portugal, Denmark, Sweden, Poland, Hungary, and Russia. The origins of these old nations lay in the early medieval era: "The long process by which in Europe sovereign states arose and nations were formed has its origins in the collapse of the Roman empire, the attempts to revive imperial power, the slow decay of the revival, and the still slower withering away of its mythology" (Seton-Watson 1977, 15). The process of formation of nations and national identities in these cases "was slow and obscure. It was a spontaneous process, not willed by anyone, though there were great events which in certain cases clearly accelerated it" (ibid., 8).

Seton-Watson's thesis echoes Renan's "Germanist" historiography, not only in its emphasis on the slow process of nation formation but also in its implicit dating. It was the failure of the Carolingian attempt to revive the Roman empire and its breakup after the Treaty of Verdun in 843 that set the stage for the growth of nations in Europe. And in spite of Susan Reynolds's criticisms of the teleological implications of Seton-Watson's narrative, that remains the temporal framework for her own analysis of medieval *regna* and of the "regnal" sentiments of their members. For Reynolds, barbarian kingdoms such as the Saxons, Lombards, Franks, Visigoths, and Anglo-Saxons also were communities of custom, law, and descent, and each sported a fabulous genealogical Trojan or biblical myth of origins. While we should not confuse them with modern nations, they shared many of the same features and functioned in similar ways (Reynolds 1983 and 1984, chap. 8; cf. Thom 1990).[12]

This is also the burden of much recent scholarship on the nature and extent of medieval collective cultural identities and sentiments. Thus, Paul Knoll (1993) documents the rise of a strong national sentiment among the nobles and clerical elites in late medieval Poland; Bruce Webster (1997) identifies a sense of Scottish national identity, again among the elites, starting in the fourteenth century after the Wars of Independence; Ulrich Im Hof (1991) describes the rise of a collective cultural identity, a Swiss national sentiment, in the Old Confederation from the late fifteenth century, when the Tell myth was first transcribed; and both Colette Beaune (1985) and Bernard Guenée (1985) record the rise of a clear sense of national identity in France (and elsewhere in Western Europe) from at least the fourteenth century.

It is, nevertheless, the English case that has stirred the greatest controversy. For most historians, an English national sentiment (as opposed to a later British sentiment) can be found no earlier than the very end of the sixteenth century.[13] But in Liah Greenfeld's massive study (1992), the date has been pushed back to the 1520s. It was in this period that the many tracts and poems of an upwardly mobile gentry revealed an identification of the English nation with the whole people, at least in sentiment and theory, that had been singularly absent in previous centuries. This was reinforced by Queen Mary's persecution of Protestants, recorded in the highly influential Foxe's *Book of Martyrs* and later by the canonical English translations of the Bible. For Greenfeld, "The birth of the English nation was not the birth of a nation, it was the birth of the nations, the birth of nationalism" (23).

Later nationalisms, starting with the French in the eighteenth century, differentiated themselves sharply from this English exemplar, adding feelings of *ressentiment* against more advanced nations to the internal competition for status mobility within the aristocratic elite (Greenfeld 1992, chap. 2).

But why should we stop at the sixteenth or even the fifteenth century? This is the question posed by Adrian Hastings (1997) in his wholesale attack on modernist historiography. For Hastings, "English post-Reformation nationalism is likely to be itself much misunderstood if it is not recognised to be just a new expression of something already well set several centuries earlier" (36).

By the fourteenth century, with the advent of Chaucerian English, we find many clear expressions of English nationalism and widespread use of a concept of the "nation" in a sense that is in all significant respects identical to the modern usage. For Hastings, England is the first great example of the nation and its nationalism. We can trace its origins right back to the Anglo-Saxon kings in their wars against the Danes; and England's nationhood in turn spurred the rise of the other Western European nations (Hastings 1997, 14–18, 36–56).

Hastings's thesis fits well into the broad category of continuous perennialism. He claims that:

1. Ethnicity is the basis of nationhood, and oral ethnicities lie at the roots of specific nations.

2. Ethnicities become nations only when they produce vernacular written literatures and are affected by "the pressures of the state" (ibid., 11).

3. The nation is a Christian phenomenon, because, of all the religions, Christianity alone sanctioned the use of vernacular languages.[14]

4. Christianity took over the Old Testament and therefore presented an image to its adherents of what a polity should be like, namely, the model of the ancient Jewish nation presented in the Old Testament.

5. The first ethnicities (apart from the Jews) to become nations were the English and their neighbors, because they were the first to produce a written vernacular literature; and when threatened, these medieval nations generated particularist nationalisms, as opposed to a later theory of nationalism.

6. The post-1789 secularizing examples are a kind of "Mark II" nationalism, and modernists have wrongly taken this later brand for the original and whole phenomenon of nationalism.

Hastings readily concedes that these post-1789 nationalisms are more numerous and are created with the help of a blueprint, the theory of nationalism. But he regards nationalist theory as relatively unimportant, because nations and nationalisms are powerfully particularist in nature. What this means for the historiography and sociology of nationalism is clear. Modernists from Kedourie and Gellner to Anderson and Hobsbawm have got it wrong: there can be, there were, premodern nations in the full sense of the term. So nations and nationalism have no necessary connection with modernization and modernity. "Understanding nations and nationalism will only be advanced when any inseparable bonding of them to the modernisation of society is abandoned" (Hastings 1997, 9). This is the nub of the present "historiographical schism" on this issue: "The key issue at the heart of our schism," claims Hastings, "lies in the date of commencement" (i.e., of nations and nationalism) (ibid.).

The date of commencement is the key issue for continuous perennialism. But this presents a difficult problem. Continuous perennialism assumes that there is a clear-cut point of origin of the nation and that the nation is also a clear-cut, homogenous unit; you either have it, or you don't. Certainly, that was how some, but not all, nationalists wanted to depict the nation, as a natural, continuing essence, even a seamless organic whole. But such a view conflicts with what we know about actual, named nations, with their many conflicts and transformations and their frequent lack of ethnic homogeneity. I am certainly not arguing that we should see the concept of the nation as a kaleidoscopic construct of present needs and interests, let alone as a mirage; it is clearly much more than that. The concept of the nation refers to a number of historical *processes*, which over time have come together and formed a distinct cultural community that may resemble, to a greater or lesser degree, the ideal type of the nation. Actual historical cases are therefore dynamic; they fluctuate and approximate to the ideal type in varying degrees.[15]

There are other difficulties with Hastings's kind of continuous perennialism. To place such weight on the creation of a literature and on written vernaculars is as restrictive as Anderson's insistence on print technology. A single vernacular language and literature undoubtedly helps to bind populations, but other factors may be equally unifying. Hastings himself cites the importance of religion, geography (especially for island nations like Britain and Ireland), and the state in welding populations into nations. His refusal to accord more importance to national*ist* ideology, which is clearly modern, reveals a failure to come to terms with the disembedding of phenomena in the modern world. Ideologies like nationalism provide blueprints for liberation and social change. They may be used by any group that so desires to legitimate and gain recognition for its collective aspirations. At the same time, nationalism can encourage and stimulate groups to seek undreamt of political goals and has often done so. (See Kedourie 1960; Hastings 1997, chap. 2.)

What of Hastings's contention that nations are a product of European Christianity and emerged in an exclusively Christian world? While he concedes the early Christian cases of the Armenians and Monophysite Amharic Ethiopians, he refuses to allow any premodern Islamic or Buddhist nations. Hastings is, in fact, quite explicit about Islam's inability to generate nations. The Islamic concept of the *umma* militates against them, and Islam's insistence on Qu'ranic Arabic precludes the sanctioning of vernaculars. And yet Islam did take over the Jewish concept of the genealogical nation, according the Arabs pride of place; while, in practice, peoples like the Persians were able to maintain their collective cultural identities after Islamization and indeed, in Firdausi's *Shahnameh*, to produce their great national (Persian) epic in the eleventh century (Frye 1966, chap. 6; see also Lewis 1970; Haim 1962, introduction).

There was an equal accommodation of world religions to existing ethnocultural communities in the Far East. Buddhism in

Burma, Tibet, and Sinhala, for example, took quite different eth-nocultural forms, helping to stimulate what Hastings might term a particularist premodern nationalism well before any stimulus from Christianity. Then there are the striking cases of China, Japan, and Korea. Did they become nations (as opposed to ethnic states) only after contact with Christianity and the Christian West and, more important, as a result of that contact? With their written vernaculars and ancient statehoods, did they not conspicuously conform to Hastings's own criteria for candidacy for nationhood (1997, 198–202)? (See also Sarkisyanz 1964; Lehmann 1982.)[16]

Recurrent Perennialism

At one point in his discussion of the English case, Adrian Hastings (1997, chap. 2) suggests that the Anglo-Saxon kingdom of King Alfred and his successors already constituted an English nation. The implication is that the Norman Conquest did little to obliterate an English sense of nationhood in the eleventh and twelfth centuries, a view supported by the medieval historian John Gillingham (1992). Other medievalists are more skeptical. Lesley Johnson (1995), for example, casts doubt on assertions about the Anglo-Saxons as a nation that forms the "true ancestor" of the modern English nation. Following her lead, we might ask, can one lose one's nationhood? Of a given population, can we legitimately ask, did they constitute a nation in a certain period, then cease to be one, only to be subsequently reconstituted as a nation, albeit in changed circumstances? And are we justified in regarding this latter nation as one and the same nation throughout history?

It is a question that has been asked of more than one nation and not only by anxious nationalists. Hastings thinks the Jews lost their nationhood, only to find it once again after two thousand years. What, then, did they constitute during the intervening period? On his criterion of a written vernacular literature, the Jews remained preeminently a nation throughout their long diaspora. Are nations without states, then, recurrent phenomena? And can the same population and culture reappear, as it were, in different epochs in the form of nations?[17]

This is the point of departure of the other main tendency, that of *recurrent perennialism*. It is an issue taken up by some ancient historians. Eduard Meyer, for example, claimed that there were only three nations in antiquity: the Greeks, the Persians, and the Jews. But were these nations in the same sense as their modern counterparts? And did they continue as nations throughout the intervening period? The alternative, entertained by some earlier historians, is to see fluctuations of nationhood in the historical record: an age of nations in Near Eastern and Greek antiquity, followed by a period of national decline and absorption of nations under the Roman empire, only to reemerge in the *regna* of the early medieval period following the barbarian migrations. The implication here is that national continuity has been broken: the ancient Egyptians, Greeks, Jews, and Persians are not the ancestors of their modern namesakes. Yet they are equally nations in the full sense of the term. (See Walek-Czernecki 1929; Koht 1947; Hadas 1950.)

Ancient Nations?

These questions of national identity and its recurrence and continuity can be best pursued by considering Meyer's three ancient nations in turn.

To take the ancient Greeks first: for Mario Attilio Levi, the ancient Greeks constituted a nation, although one rent by divisions between different *poleis*; Hellas constituted the ideal and figured prominently in the rhetoric of Greek statesmen and intellectuals, most famously in Herodotus's *History of the Persian Wars* and Pericles' *Funeral Oration* of 430 B.C.E., which held out a vision of Athens as an "education to Greece" (Levi 1965).

On the other hand, Moses Finley, using Meinecke's distinction between *Kulturnation* and *Staatsnation*, denied to the ancient Greeks any sense or conception of political nationhood. Contrasting Hesiod's *Works and Days*, with its lament over the fifth, the iron, age of man, with Jeremiah's prophecies of doom, Finley writes: "The Hebrew prophet had one and only one point of reference, his people, his nation, while the Greek poet had several, of which his nation was not one. The moment he left the daily concerns of his farmers to consider more universal matters, he leaped from the community to the human race" (Finley 1986, 126).

Ancient Greek political loyalties were focused exclusively on the *polis*; any other identity or loyalty was familial or cultural but always apolitical. But this stark contrast has to be qualified. Political loyalties also could be marshaled by ethnic solidarities—Ionian, Aeolian, Dorian, and Boeotian—which signified far more than Greek dialects. Ionians and Dorians, for example, had different calendars, games, family rituals, tribal organizations, and building styles; and appeals to these ethnic networks could mobilize mass political sentiments in the Peloponnesian War. Besides, there did exist in ancient Greece a political sentiment of Panhellenism, though it seems to have been confined to a small elite, including the philosopher Isocrates. This anti-Persian Hellenic sentiment had been stimulated by the Persian wars; and though some cities had submitted during Xerxes' invasion, the Greek resistance at Marathon, Salamis, and Plataea had kindled a lively Hellenic sentiment, which pervaded not only drama, historiography, and the visual arts but had political consequences such as the Delian League. Edith Hall's recent study has shown how the climate that produced Aeschylus's *Persae* also led to the "invention" of the "barbarian" Other and a growing sense of the political boundedness of the "civilized" Greek world (Fondation Hardt 1962; Alty 1982; Finley 1986, chap. 7; E. Hall 1992).[18]

If it is unclear how far ancient Greeks constituted a nation, as opposed to an ethnic community, an even greater question mark hangs over their relationship with modern Greeks. Most scholars follow Jacob Fallmereyer in denying what is still an article of faith among most contemporary Greeks, that they are the lineal descendants of the Greeks of classical antiquity. Given the massive migrations of Avars, Slavs, and Albanians into mainland Greece from the sixth century C.E., which pushed the existing Greek population to the coasts and islands, the population of modern Greece is likely to be as ethnically heterogeneous as most other modern nations. Even if it is not possible to prove that modern Greeks are *not* descended from the Greeks of classical antiquity, the fact that it was only in the tenth century that mainland Greece was reconquered and re-Christianized by Byzantium must make us treat assertions of Greek ancestral continuity with caution (Campbell and Sherrard 1968, chap. 1; Just 1989).

A more promising line of inquiry focuses on cultural rather than demographic criteria: whether we can trace Greek cultural and symbolic continuities through the medieval epoch into modern times. For Paschalis Kitromilides the answer is clear: we can speak only of reappropriations by modern Greek intellectuals of elements of the classical heritage. Even the Byzantine legacy was not taken up until its canonization in the monumental five-volume *History of the Greek Nation*, written by Konstantinos Paparrigopoulos in the mid-nineteenth century. Kitromilides underlines the novelty of Paparrigopoulos's idea of the Greek nation as a collective actor, persisting and acting from antiquity through the Byzantine era into the modern epoch; for, until the nineteenth century, Greece and Greeks were subsumed in the far-flung Orthodox *ecumene*, as they had earlier been in the polyethnic and polyglot Byzantine empire (Kitromilides 1979, 1998; Mango 1980, chap. 1).

Against this view, it is still possible to identify some cultural continuities. Kitromilides himself alludes to some of them, when he mentions "inherited forms of cultural expression, such as those associated with the Orthodox liturgical cycle and the images of emperors, the commemoration of Christian kings, the evocation of the Orthodox kingdom and its earthly seat, Constantinople, which is so powerfully communicated in texts such as the Akathist Hymn, sung every year during Lent and forming such an intimate component of Orthodox worship . . ." (Kitromilides 1998, 31).

There are other lines of Greek continuity. Despite the adoption of a new religion, Christianity, certain traditions, such as a dedication to competitive values, have remained fairly constant, as have the basic forms of the Greek language and the contours of the Greek homeland (though its center of gravity was subject to change). And John Armstrong has pointed to the "precocious nationalism" that took hold of the Greek population of the Byzantine Empire under the last Palaeologan emperors and that was directed as much against the Catholic Latins as against the Muslim Turks—an expression of medieval Greek national sentiment as well as a harbinger of later Greek nationalism. But again, we may ask: was this Byzantine sentiment a case of purely confessional loyalty or of ethnoreligious nationalism? (See Armstrong 1982, 174–81; cf. Baynes and Moss 1969, 119–27, and Carras 1983.)

If long-term Greek cultural continuity is uncertain, what of the Persians? Once again, names, basic Farsi linguistic forms, and the concentration of Farsi speakers in their homeland on the Iranian plateau exhibit a considerable measure of overall continuity, at least since the Sassanids, despite the intervening Islamization of the population. And once again, there is plenty of evidence of a desire by modern Iranian elites to reappropriate different aspects and periods of a "Persian"—some would say "Aryan"—past. But on the Iranian plateau, with its many ethnic communities and religions, even more than in the Greek valleys, it is hard to find clear evidence of a Persian national identity in premodern eras, except perhaps among a small archaizing Zoroastrian elite under Chosroes II in the sixth century. This is not to say there was no sense of ethnocultural difference between Persians and their neighbors. For Richard Frye, indeed, a Persian cultural identity was strong enough to reshape its adopted religion, Islam, and impose on its conquerors much of its own culture. This could be seen both in New Persian poetry and in Firdausi's great epic, the *Shahnameh* (Book of kings), with its central myth of the conflict between Iran and Tur'an and its recital of the exploits of the Persian and Zoroastrian Sassanid kings and heroes (Frye 1966, chap. 6; *Cambridge History of Iran* 1983, vol. 3, part 1, chaps. 3–4 and vol. 4, chap. 1).[19]

It is not till the sixteenth century, however, that a greater measure of Persian solidarity and cohesion can be discerned. For the next two centuries, the Safavid dynasty sought increasingly to unify and identify the state with the Shi'ite form of Islam. But with the arrival of the Qajjar Afghan dynasty, the sense of Persian national continuity was again broken; and it was only in reaction to British and Russian imperialism and later, during the modern Pahlavi period, that conscious attempts were made to reappropriate aspects of the Persian past and build a Persian national identity while ruling a polyethnic Iran. As a result, a Persian national identity appears to be even more elusive and fluctuating than the Greek case, or is this just a reflection of the paucity of relevant sources? (See Avery 1965; Cottam 1979, chaps. 2–3, 10–13; Keddie 1981, chaps. 1–3.)

We are, it seems, on firmer documentary ground with the Jewish case. For Hastings, as we saw, the ancient Jews constituted the model of the nation, and this appears to be supported by the sociological analysis of the Old Testament scholar Steven Grosby. From roughly the late seventh century B.C.E., he argues, Israel appears as a fully fledged nation. The prophetic movement and the Deuteronomic reforms had helped to create a pervasive belief, certainly among the elites, in "all Israel" living in its own sacred land and worshipping a single god, Yahweh, in a prescribed center, Jerusalem. For Grosby, the belief in the existence of a "people" living in a specific trans-local but bounded territory is vital for the existence of a nation: "This conjoining (sc. of a people to a land) is a characteristic referent in the shared beliefs constitutive of nationality, ancient and modern: a people has its land and a land has its people" (Grosby 1991, 240).

Of course, Israel was not the only collectivity in the ancient Near East to develop such beliefs. According to Grosby, we find such designations conflating land and people among the Armenians and perhaps the Edomites, with the result that we can be fairly certain of their sense of a collective cultural and political identity. Similar designations also can be found in ancient Egypt: attachment to the native land is evident in the "Song of Sinuhe," as well as in the words of the Pharaoh Kamose to his council in Thebes around 1580 B.C.E.:

I should like to know for what purpose is my strength. One prince sits in Avaris and another in Nubia, and here sit I together with an Asiatic and a Nubian, each one having his slice of Egypt . . . I will grapple with him, and rip open his belly. My desire is to save Egypt which the Asiatics have smitten. . . . Your counsel is wrong and I will fight with the Asiatics. . . . Men shall say of me in Thebes: Kamose, protector of Egypt. (Grosby 1991, 247, citing Wilson 1951, 164).[20]

Here, too, the idea that the land of Egypt belongs only to the Egyptians, associated with the ascendancy of a supreme god of the land—here Amon-Re of Thebes—is indicative of a belief in the existence of an Egyptian nation. This conjunction of beliefs is even more clearly illustrated in the case of ancient Israel:

It was precisely these factors—the constitutive prominence of the "land" and the "people" in the worship of Yahweh, and a law the jurisdiction of which was conceived to be both that land and that people—which were absent in the histories of the ancient Greeks and the Aramean city-kingdoms. Equally important in the formation of ancient Israel as a nation was that ancient Israel had a center, Jerusalem, to which "all Israel" could and did look. No such center existed in ancient Greece. In the case of "all

Aram," Damascus was prevented by the Assyrians from developing into its center. (Ibid., 242)

In a later article, however, Grosby is less sure about the status of the Aramean kingdoms. While clearly not a national state, the designation "all Aram," the supremacy of the god Hadad in their pantheon, their common Aramean language, and the fact that both they themselves and the Israelites, whom they so often fought, appeared to consider that all the Arameans were "ethnically related" suggests a growing awareness of common Aramean nationality (Grosby 1997, 15).

I cite this case because it illustrates the problems and uncertainties surrounding the question of the historical dating of nations. There are, in the first place, the problems of paucity and interpretation of sources, particularly from the ancient world. Allied to this is the question of historical context and the dangers of reading quite different epochs in the light of later concepts and preoccupations, to which I shall return. But beyond these considerations lies the problematic nature of sociological categorization itself. Grosby himself remarks, apropos of his analysis of ancient Edom, Aram, and Armenia:

An examination of these three collectivities poses point blank both the question of whether or not nations existed in the ancient Near East and, correspondingly, the problem of the application of the category of nationality to these collectivities. An analysis of these three cases further reminds us that in reality the boundaries separating the categories which we employ in our investigations of various collectivities, ancient and modern, are permeable. Rarely does a collectivity correspond with exactitude to a particular analytic category. This is true not only for the collectivities of antiquity, but for the modern national state as well. (Ibid., 2)

This does not mean that we should abandon the attempt to fashion analytic categories to demarcate different kinds of collectivity, ancient as well as modern. Rather, it requires us to spell out clearly the components of each category in relation to others of the same general kind: in this case, nations in relation to city-states, empires, and tribes.[21]

Thus, speaking of Armenia in the fourth and fifth centuries of the common era, Grosby documents terms which suggest "two referents of the collective self-consciousness constitutive of a nation of Armenia, a relation of a bounded areal jurisdiction, a territory, and a language . . . which was seen as common to Armenians in their territory" (ibid., 21). To this we may add a belief in the common ancestry of all Armenians. (See also Suny 1993a.)

This same problem of categories reappears at a later stage of Israel's history. For many modern historians it has become common to assume the existence of a Jewish nation and nationalism in the Second Temple period. S. G. F. Brandon, for example, regarded the Zealot revolt from 6 C.E. to the fall of Jerusalem as a nationalist guerrilla movement on behalf of the nation of Israel in its divinely promised land and argued that Jesus and his followers were at least sympathetic to the Zealots and the Jewish nationalist cause. Roman economic oppression and religious insensitivity combined to drive many Jews into the arms of the Zealot nationalists even before the Great Revolt of 66–70 C.E. Even if they cannot accept Brandon's portrait of a revolutionary-nationalist Jesus, many scholars would concur with his thesis about ancient Jewish nationalism in Roman Palestine (Brandon 1967, chap. 2; cf. Zeitlin 1988, chap. 10).[22]

Similarly, the earlier Maccabean revolt against the Seleucid monarch, Antiochus Epiphanes, was premised on the existence not just of a separate Jewish religious community but of a distinct Jewish nation whose survival the forced hellenization of Judea was endangering. This is the position adopted by Victor Tcherikover, as it was also the underlying assumption of the vivid account given by the late Professor Menahem Stern. Stern (1971) argued that the events leading up to the Maccabean revolt were unusual in ancient history because "they involved the total religious persecution of an entire nation" (92). The elevation of Menelaus to High Priest opened a new page in relations "between the Seleucid kingdom and the Jewish nation" (95). Stern further speaks about the "great majority of the nation remaining faithful to their ancestral religion" to the point of mass martyrdom, which "served as an example to both Jews and non-Jews in all generations to come" (98). The Hasmonean resistance ensured the "later development of the Jewish nation," for the ideals of the Torah had penetrated "the broad masses of the nation" (99). Stern also speaks of a "struggle over the religious and ethnic character of the majority of the country's rural population" ending "with a victory for the Jews" (101); of the "long-standing hopes" for "the restoration of Israel's glory" (ibid.); of the Hasmonean house being carried on "the waves of national-religious enthusiasm" (105); and finally of the Maccabean rebellion being a "war of national liberation" and serving as "a symbol for future generations" (106). (See also Tcherikover 1970.)

As an analysis of events in second-century B.C.E. Judea, all this may be both logical and persuasive. But it assumes exactly what is to be demonstrated, namely, that there was indeed in existence at this time an ancient Jewish nation and a Jewish nationalism, in a sense similar to a modern Jewish nation and nationalism in Israel or indeed to any other modern nation and nationalism. This would also seem to be the view adopted by Doron Mendels in *The Rise and Fall of Jewish Nationalism*, an account of the main factors of ancient Jewish political nationalism from Judas Maccabeus to Bar-Kochba. Mendels's objective is to "understand Jewish nationalism within the context of the nationalism of the Hellenistic world." He explains this by claiming that "the nations of the ancient Near East that were the neighbours of the Jews had specific and well-defined symbols of political nationalism, namely, the temple, territory, kingship, and the army" (Mendels 1992, 1).

These symbols of a political nationalism can be traced throughout the period (from 200 B.C.E. to 135 C.E.), unlike "the more general facets of nationalism, such as the calendar, the law and the language" (ibid., 2). Mendels contends that "every religious Jew who believed in the scriptures had nationalistic ideas," and, taking their cue from the Bible, this meant a national state. At the same time, "the majority of the Jews had a 'passive' kind of nationalism" that became active only during crises (ibid., 3).[23]

All this would suggest that Doron Mendels, like Menahem Stern and Steven Grosby, embraces a perennialist view of nations and nationalism, of the recurrent kind, according to which a Jewish nation and nationalism has emerged at various points in history from biblical antiquity to present-day Israel. But the question then arises whether the ancient Jewish nation bears any resemblance to the modern one. Here, Mendels introduces a note of caution when he warns:

Can one speak of nationalism in the ancient world? Yes, but not in the sense it has in modern times. . . . By and large, there is a major question whether one can use the modern models and descriptions of nationalism proposed by distinguished historians and sociologists like E. Kedourie, E. Gellner and A. D. Smith in any discussion about antiquity. Thus I would not even risk entering the area of definitions of nationalism in the Hellenistic age. Instead this chapter will merely attempt to describe how the Hellenistic world coped with the issue of *ethnicity*, which will for convenience here be called "nationalism." (Ibid., 13, my italics)

In other words, where Mendels (and perhaps others) have been using the term *nationalism*, we should really understand that they mean *ethnicity*—a procedure justified on the grounds that "scholars of antiquity use terms that have been used to describe other later phenomena," like *imperialism* or *utopia* (ibid., 13). Mendels contends that, in the Hellenistic period, "nationalistic traits . . . can be discerned in many *ethne* (peoples) of the Hellenistic world, traits that distinguish them from one another. Perhaps the most important factor is that the various peoples of the ancient world were aware of how they differed in terms of language, territory, history, culture, and religion" (ibid., 13–14).

But is a sense of cultural and historical difference the same as "nationalism"? Can the perception of differences even in political symbols like temple, territory, and kingship be usefully termed nationalism? Or must we accept different concepts of nationalism in different epochs and culture areas? By refusing to enter the arena of definitions, Mendels leaves such questions unanswered, while hinting at these very possibilities.

These are, in many ways, the central problems of our historiographical inquiry. But they are, if anything, exacerbated by the allied question of Jewish continuity: whether the Jews lost their nationhood for two thousand years, along with their homeland, or whether it is possible to trace a distinctive Jewish nation or at least a sense of distinctive Jewish nationhood back to the medieval or even ancient epochs. This was certainly the assumption of many modern Jewish and Zionist historians, from Graetz and Dubnow to Ben-Zion Dinur. They all thought in terms of an enduring community called the "Jewish people," whose character and achievements could be traced from biblical antiquity to the present (Pinson 1960; cf. Hertzberg 1960, introduction, and Akzin 1964).[24]

This interpretation of Jewish history, which has recently been challenged by the "post-Zionist" new historians and sociologists, combines both kinds of perennialism and invites the possibility of a metaphysical rather than a purely causal historical analysis. For it suggests that not only is the Jewish nation a visibly recurrent collective cultural identity over a three-thousand-year span, it is also one that endured immemorially throughout the long exile of its dispersion and fragmentation. And much the same could be argued on behalf of the diaspora existence and national revival of the Armenian and Greek nations, albeit over shorter time spans (Suny 1993a; A. D. Smith 1995c; Ram 1998).

Conclusion: Problems with Perennialism

Just these nations figure prominently in the work of John Armstrong, whose major volume, *Nations before Nationalism*, combines both versions of perennialism. On the one hand, Armstrong provides a matrix of premodern long- and medium-term factors leading to the gradual emergence of modern national identity. On the other hand, the body of the book deals not with nations but with ethnic identities in medieval Islam and Christendom. For Armstrong it would seem that ethnicity and nationhood are identical, that "nations" are recurrent throughout history, and that some of them at least can boast a continuous history of some centuries, if not millennia. So, presumably, Armstrong would regard the Jewish and Armenian nations as perennial in both senses of the term, existing continuously from antiquity in their diasporas and recurring in a territorial-national form after a long caesura (Armstrong 1982, esp. chap. 7, 1997).[25]

I do not think this conflation of ethnicity and nationalism, on the one hand, and continuous and recurrent nationhood, on the other hand, is helpful to an understanding of the problem of nations and nationalism and their role in history. It seems to obscure and further confuse an already complex and difficult conceptual and historical problem. Nevertheless, it has the merit of bringing us up against the fundamental issues in the elucidation of the role of nations and nationalism in history. These include the following problems:

1. *The question of definition* of the concept of the nation and the need for clear definitions of key terms to allow us to proceed in a discriminating manner. For modernists, nations are assumed to be "mass phenomena," in Walker Connor's words, involving a common citizenship for all members, at least in theory. For

perennialists, such a definition appears too restrictive. For Hastings, it is enough that a large number of people outside the ruling elite believe they constitute a separate nation and act accordingly. But exactly what proportion of such people suffices to define the existence of a nation? And is this belief and action enough to decide the issue of nation formation (Connor 1994, chap. 8; Hastings 1997, 26)?

2. *The question of the historical context* of collective cultural identities. Here the modernists insist on the autonomy of each historical epoch and accuse the perennialists of importing ideas and concepts from the modern into earlier epochs. Hence, their rejection of any form of "retrospective nationalism." This is the burden of John Breuilly's refusal to allow any form of nationalism before the eighteenth century, despite a superficial similarity of terms, and of Susan Reynolds's insistence on describing and analyzing each epoch in terms of its own concepts rather than those of later epochs. But this still leaves us with questions about "things" rather than "words," that is, with how different the earlier types of collective cultural identities and political actions were from the later kinds and wherein lie the differences (Breuilly 1993, 3–5; Reynolds 1983).

3. *The question of teleology,* which is closely allied to this issue. We saw how Susan Reynolds took Hugh Seton-Watson to task for portraying the history of modern nations in terms of an inexorable movement from their rudimentary beginnings in the early medieval epoch to the almost predetermined present-day nation-states. In other words, it is quite misleading to see medieval polities as embryonic modern nations. But does this rule out a search for the nation's origins? Does it not require an equal act of faith in the novelty of nations, sprung fully armed, if not from the head of Zeus, then from the heads of the enlighteners (Reynolds 1984, chap. 8)?

What all this suggests is the need for an approach that does justice to the character of different types of collective cultural identities in each epoch, while charting the overall relationship between their different kinds. These are some of the themes and issues that I hope to address when I outline an ethnosymbolic approach to the problem of the role of nations and nationalism in history.

3 Social Construction and Ethnic Genealogy

In the past two decades the idea of the nation as a text to be narrated and an artifact and construct to be deconstructed has gained wide currency. For all its relativist and postmodernist subtexts, this remains essentially a modernist perspective and one that often has a post-Marxist lineage. At the same time, it seeks to go beyond modernism to encompass an era of "postmodernity"; and because it sees nations and nationalism as phenomena intrinsic to modernity, it predicts the imminent demise of both as we move into a postmodern, global era.

The viewpoints that can be grouped under this postmodern rubric are many and varied. But they all share a fundamental belief in the socially constructed quality of the nation and nationalism. This is why I find it useful to refer to them as "constructionist" approaches or perspectives. The basic ideas of social constructionism include the following:

1. The assumption that nationalism created and continues to create nations, rather than the opposite

2. The belief that nations are recent and novel products of modernity, so far sharing the modernist view

3. A view of nations as social constructs and cultural artifacts deliberately engineered by elites

4. The idea that nationalists "invent" and "imagine" the nation by representing it to the majority through a variety of cultural media and social rituals

5. The belief that only in modern conditions is such invention and imagination possible and likely

6. A sense of the supersession of the age of nations along with that of modernity in a more globalizing epoch.

Novel in this view, in contrast to the more political and sociological versions of modernism, are the elements of cultural representation and social engineering and the importance of deliberate elite innovation that this implies. Nations, in these views, are the product of "cultural work" on the part of elites; without that cultural work, without such elite narratives, the nation is unimaginable and incommunicable.[1]

Invented Traditions, Imagined Communities

Perhaps the most literal and influential of these constructionist schemes is that presented by Eric Hobsbawm and his associates. They regard the nation as a creation of nationalism and hence entirely novel and recent. For Hobsbawm himself, the age of nationalism, despite the example of the French Revolution, commences around 1830 with an inclusive mass-democratic and political nationalism of the large nations, followed after 1870 by a divisive, ethnolinguistic and often right-wing nationalism of small nations (Hobsbawm 1990, chap. 4).

It is in this latter era that we witness a proliferation of *invented traditions* of the nation—statuomania, sporting contests, national festivals, and the like (Hobsbawm and Ranger 1983, chap. 7). Unlike their earlier counterparts, these recent invented traditions are deliberate and invariant creations. They do not adapt and evolve, like customs and traditions in preindustrial societies. They are sociopolitical constructs forged, even fabricated, by cultural engineers, who design symbols, mythologies, rituals, and histories specifically to meet modern mass needs. Not only were entirely new symbols, like flags and anthems, created but also "historic continuity had to be invented, for example by creating an ancient past beyond effective historical continuity, either by semi-fiction (Boadicea, Vercingetorix, Arminius the Cheruscan) or by forgery (Ossian, the medieval Czech manuscripts)" (Hobsbawm and Ranger 1983, 7). These constructs make up a large part of what we mean by nations and national identities; therefore, the study of invented traditions is, Hobsbawm claims,

highly relevant to that comparatively recent innovation, the "nation," with its associated phenomena: nationalism, the nation-state, national symbols, histories and the rest. All these rest on exercises in social engineering which are often deliberate and always innovative, if only because historical novelty implies innovation. Israeli and Palestinian nationalism and nations must be novel, whatever the historic continuities of Jews and Middle Eastern Muslims, since the very concept of territorial states of the currently standard type in their region was barely thought of a century ago, and hardly became a serious prospect before the end of World War I. (Ibid., 13–14)[2]

Now these invented traditions emerged and were disseminated in a period of mass democracy and mobilization consequent on large-scale urbanization and industrialization. In Western Europe and America such conditions prevailed after 1870, and that is why ruling classes were compelled to invent traditions that would channel and control the energies and aspirations of the newly enfranchised masses. In fact, the invented traditions of the nation turned out to be far and away the most potent and durable instrument of social control (Hobsbawm and Ranger 1983, chap. 1). But after the excesses of the Second World War and the Cold War confrontation, the growth of vast globalizing forces—transnational economic units, huge power blocs, international organizations, mass migration, and mass communications—has undermined the efficacy of the nation-state and rendered its boundaries obsolete, despite the temporary proliferation of divisive ethnic nationalisms. In these circumstances we may begin to celebrate the supersession of nationalism. "The owl of Minerva which brings wisdom, said Hegel, flies out at dusk. It is a good sign that it is now circling round nations and nationalism" (Hobsbawm 1990, 183).

I shall return later to the owl of Minerva. For the moment we may ask, what exactly are these invented traditions and why do they exercise such a powerful appeal? Hobsbawm, Ranger, and their associates give as examples the rebuilding of the British Houses of Parliament in 1849 in the Gothic style; the modern (i.e., Victorian) provenance of the British coronation ceremony; the modern origin of the Scottish kilt, as well as of the cult of the Highlands; the nineteenth-century institution of archery societies and contests in Switzerland in honor and imitation of the alleged feat of William Tell; and the late-eighteenth-century institution of the Eisteddfod in Wales. These are all modern inventions that pretend to a deep historical continuity with a distant past that is largely spurious (Hobsbawm and Ranger 1983).

But is it so spurious? What does Hobsbawm mean by a "deep" or an "effective historical continuity"? And does that actually matter? For a study of nations and nationalism and their role in history, how important is the documented truth content of nationalist rediscoveries, as against their memory content? Conversely, is not the quality of living memory in a population more critical for the meaning and success of a nationalist enterprise than any amount of well-documented but unresonating evidence? I am not arguing the relativist position that historical truth content is irrelevant to the nationalist enterprise. Clearly, the ability of professional historians to document lies and explode pure fictions is an important element in the manifold relationships between past, present, and future on which a national community is based. But it is only one of several elements; and it must be balanced by other factors, such as the energizing force of myths, the resonance of shared memories, and the vivid appeal of symbols, all of which carry across generations to establish a chain of felt and willed continuity.[3]

This point is very clearly illustrated by the essay on the rediscovery of the Welsh past by Prys Morgan in the Hobsbawm and Ranger volume. Far from confirming the "invented tradition" thesis, Morgan shows how the Welsh exiles in London who decided to revive the festival of the *Eisteddfod* in 1789 returned to the poetic and musical traditions of the ancient Welsh bardic contests, which had only recently died out in the countryside taverns (the "almanack contests"), and gave them a new form. True, they appended completely unhistorical decorative elements like the Druidic *Gorsedd*, in a kind of romantic Ossianic flourish; but the core of the modern poetic and musical festival, celebrated to this day, is the original bardic contest, which, like the ancient festivals going back to 1176, conforms strictly to its complex medieval metrical forms while adapting the themes of the poems that they recite to modern conditions (Morgan 1983).

Hobsbawm's approach has undoubtedly proved influential. Following his lead, the Swiss historian Georg Kreis has sought to demonstrate how the elaborate celebration of the Swiss National Day was "invented" by the federal authorities in 1891 to commemorate the six-hundredth anniversary of the swearing of the oath of the three forest cantons on the Rütli meadow overlooking Lake Lucerne. Indeed, they even rewrote Swiss foundation history, changing the traditional date of 1307 to the new date of 1291, as described in the rediscovered *Bundesbrief* of the Everlasting Alliance of that year and so memorably depicted in Heinrich Füssli's Michelangelesque *Oath of the Rütli* 1778–81), commissioned by the Zurich Rathaus (Rosenblum 1967, chap. 2; Kreis 1991).[4]

Similarly, the Greek historian Paschalis Kitromilides has shown how recent was the *Megale Idea* which came to dominate Greek national aspirations. For it was not till the mid-nineteenth century that Byzantium and its imperial tradition was incorporated into Greek national consciousness. Till then, under the influence of Korais, classical Hellenism had pervaded the consciousness of the Greek intelligentsia and their merchant allies. Only after 1850 did the great historian Paparrigopoulos reshape Greek historical tradition and national consciousness through his demonstration of the genius of the Greek nation in its greatest achievement, Byzantine civilization. Indeed, "as a 'Byzantine idea' the Great Idea was a latecomer to Greek politics, never commanded universal acceptance among the political class and was rather short-lived" (Kitromilides 1998, 33).[5]

Israelis, too, it appears, have had their share in the invention of tradition. According to Yael Zerubavel, elements of the Zionist consciousness, like the veneration of Trumpeldor and Tel Hai and the cult of the Zealots of Masada, can be viewed as recent invented traditions serving the immediate needs of Zionist pioneering elites in the 1920s and 1930s as they sought to portray an activist, heroic "new Jew" in Palestine—in contrast to the burdened and victimized "old Jew" of the diasporic exile. Similarly, the post-Zionist "new historians" and "critical sociologists," like Ilan Pappe, Gershon Shafir, and Uri Ram, have argued that the Zionist enterprise itself was the creation of an exclusive pioneering Ashkenazi settler elite who invented a new historical consciousness of the unitary "Jewish people" and institutionalized it in the recently founded state and its national education system (Zerubavel 1995; Shafir 1989; Ram 1995, 1998).[6]

One could go further. One could show that the very concept of the nation as a substantial, enduring community is a reification based on state nationalizing practices and events. According to Rogers Brubaker and the "new institutionalism" in sociology, this is very much what the Soviet leaders contrived in the former Soviet Union—engineering languages and ethnicities, sometimes in a parody of Herder's and Engels's linguistic assumptions—and it was these ethnolinguistic units that often became the bases for the post-Soviet ethnic republics. So it is not "nations without nationalism" but "nationalism without nations" that we need to analyze and thereby cease to treat the state-created effect called nations as a causal factor or substantial entity (Brubaker 1996, 21).

But this, surely, is the ultimate *reductio ad absurdum* of our inquiry. It is difficult, on this logic, to see why we should credit the "state" with any more reality and substance than the nation. Constructing the nation away misses the central point about historical nations: their powerfully felt and willed presence, the feeling shared among so many people of belonging to a transgenerational community of history and destiny. We do not have to reify the nation by conceding the vivid tangibility and felt power of its presence, irrespective of the way in which the nation or any particular nations emerged. (See A. D. Smith 1998, 76–77; see also McCrone 1998, 3–4.)

In my view, all these accounts raise more questions than they answer. In what sense are these national traditions and practices, cults and commemorations, "invented"? What exactly do we mean by this multifaceted term? Doesn't Benedict Anderson have a point when he accuses Ernest Gellner—and we might add Hobsbawm and his many followers—of assimilating "'invention' to 'fabrication' and 'falsehood', rather than to 'imagining' and 'creation'"? The idea that nationalists or other elites fabricated national cultural artifacts that, once deconstructed and delegitimated and their artificiality and hybridity revealed, will fragment and melt in the fires of globalization seems remote from historical and contemporary fact. Rather, we must ask, why are so many of these cultural artifacts so successful? How do we account for their character and resilience? Why, in the first place, are they felt to be necessary? For even Hobsbawm concedes that such conscious invented tradition succeeded "mainly in proportion to its success in broadcasting on a wavelength to which the public was ready to tune in" (Hobsbawm and Ranger 1983, 263; Anderson 1991, 6).[7]

This is where that other great postmodern concept, the *imagined political community*, is so enlightening. Anderson's account, like Hobsbawm's, has Marxist underpinnings. This is most obviously visible in the motive power attributed to "print capitalism" in the dissemination of printed books and newspapers from the sixteenth century on and the rise of anonymous reading publics to whom and for whom the imagined community of the nation is represented and purveyed. Yet it is the idea of the nation as an imagined political community and hence as a cultural artifact, at once sovereign, finite, and horizontally cross-class and moving along linear, "empty homogenous time," that has so tangibly caught the postmodernist scholarly fancy (Anderson 1991, chaps. 1–3; cf. Bhabha 1990, chap. 16).

In fact, we often find this idea detached from its Andersonian moorings. It has become a topos of the literary imagination, a metaphor for the constructed quality of all communities. But for Anderson himself, the idea of the imagined political community was historically embedded. For print capitalism could begin to create the basis for the imagined community of the nation only when certain conditions had been met. These included the basic fatalities of fear of death and oblivion and global linguistic diversity; the underlying conditions of a decline of sacred monarchies and cosmological script communities; and a revolution in our ideas of time, in which simultaneous, messianic time is replaced by linear, homogeneous time measured by clock and calendar.

But, like Hobsbawm, Anderson overplays the ruptures with premodern societies and cultures. As the medieval historian Lesley Johnson has pointed out, time in the Middle Ages was not only conceived of as messianic; people had clear linear conceptions of time, as, we may add, did some ancient peoples like the Jews and Greeks. Similarly, modern nationalisms have, as Anderson himself demonstrates in his discussion of the "official nationalisms" of Japan and Russia, benefited from the attentions of imperial monarchs, churches, and religious dignitaries. How else can we explain the spate of radical "religious nationalisms" in so many parts of the modern world, whose shrill resurgence and mass mobilizing power in Asia and Africa, as well as in Europe, Mark Juergensmeyer has recently charted? (See Johnson 1995; Juergensmeyer 1993; cf. D. E. Smith 1974.)

The complex relations between these imagined new communities of the nation and older religious communities is explored in another richly documented essay by Paschalis Kitromilides, revealingly entitled "'Imagined Communities' and the Origins of the National Question in the Balkans" (1989). Here, Kitromilides attempts to demonstrate the total novelty of the late-eighteenth- and early-nineteenth-century conception of secular Greek, Serb, Bulgarian, and Rumanian nations, which replaced the former large-scale Byzantine Orthodox *ecumene*. These newly imagined communities marked a complete break with older identities, however much they sought to link themselves with older traditions in the area. They were the products of the imaginations of the intelligentsia and later of the state elites that took power in these newly formed communities. But this is only part of the story. Orthodoxy did not simply wither away, to be replaced by secular Greek, Bulgar, or Serb nationalisms. Rather, the latter coexisted with and drew upon the myths, symbols, and traditions of the former; indeed, the creation of separate ethnic exarchates and the influence of the Orthodox liturgies and priesthoods marked crucial stages in the evolution of these nationalisms. The Greek war of independence was fought as much between Muslim and Orthodox Christian as between the newly imagined communities of Turks and Greeks, and echoes of this were found in the philhellenic West—for example, in Delacroix's great protest against the suffering of the Greeks in *The Massacre of Chios* (1824). (See Campbell and Sherrard 1968, chap. 1; Roudometov 1998.)[8]

It is, of course, perfectly true that the nation as a community of people, most of whom will never know or meet one another, is an imagined community. But as Anderson points out, so is every community above the face-to-face level. More important, the nation is equally a *felt* and a *willed* community. Emphasizing imagination as the key attribute of the nation overlooks these other vital dimensions of will and emotion. Long ago, the psalmist sang:

> How shall we sing the Lord's song in a strange land?
> If I forget thee, O Jerusalem, Let my right hand forget its cunning;
> Let my tongue cleave to the roof of my mouth, If I prefer not
> Jerusalem above my chief joy.
>
> Ps. 137:4–6)

The psalmist does not reason: "I must imagine myself in the homeland, and then sing the Lord's song"; rather he declares, "I must love my homeland and sacrifice my 'chief joy' for her." Above imagination, the psalmist places emotion and will, devotion and purpose. Equally, for the ancient Greeks who died fighting the Persians, it was not a question of imagining a noble and disinterested homeland, as Anderson suggests in his attempt to explain mass national self-sacrifice. It was a matter of love for and duty to their beloved city and homeland. As Simonides' epitaph on Leonidas and his three hundred at Thermopylae so aptly expressed it,

> Go, passer-by, tell the Spartans that here,
> Obedient to their laws, we lie.

The imagined national community is a moral community and a sacred communion, demanding sacrifices from all its members.

These are the very dimensions of nationalism that even so eminent a world historian as William McNeill overlooks. For McNeill, human history is marked by three stages. The first, premodern epoch, was marked by polyethnic hierarchies of skilled labor. These hierarchies created the great civilizations out of their much-sought-out skills, and civilized communities were accordingly polyglot and polyethnic. In the second stage, from 1750 to 1914, a unique combination of factors nourished the age of nations; the classicism of the intelligentsia, the new conscript armies, the new reading publics, and the ability to replenish from an ethnically homogeneous countryside labor skills depleted by disease. Together, these factors fed the dream of national unity and cultural homogeneity (McNeill 1986, chaps. 1–2). But by the mid-twentieth century their power had waned, and the dream of national unity, which in any case was largely a mirage, faded. Now we are once again returning to looser transnational economies and cultures based on the old polyethnic hierarchies of skill. As McNeill sums it up: "Polyethnic hierarchy is on the rise, everywhere." Like the cultural critic Homi Bhabha and the historian of India, Partha Chatterjee, McNeill envisages a much more fragmented and hybridized society as we move into a postnational era, largely as a result of large-scale immigration and mass communications. The contemporary scene is essentially fragmented and cosmopolitan; it has no place for communities of devotion and purpose, for the moral community or the sacred communion of the nation (McNeill 1986, 82; cf. Bhabha 1990, chap. 16; Chatterjee 1993, chap. 1; Soysal 1994).

A Critique of Social Constructionism

But can we really uphold this fundamentally postnational vision of the nation?

Central to the many varieties of social constructionism is the idea of the nation as a malleable and modern cultural artifact. So malleable, indeed, that we look in vain for clear definitions of the nation and nationalism. There is also a lack of sociological solidity in these conceptions. Unlike the classical modernists, such as Deutsch and Gellner, social constructionists treat the nation as a narrative text or a cultural artifact that, once deconstructed, dissolves into its component ethnic parts; or alternatively, like Rogers Brubaker, they reject altogether any notion of the nation as a real community. But why, in that case, should so many people continue to define themselves as a living and substantial national community or choose to lay down their lives for an elite construct and artifact, even after it has been deconstructed by the postmodernists? As Michael Billig has shown, the ideas of nation and home are deeply embedded in our language and everyday practices, suggesting a social reality that cannot be easily dissolved. The same applies to the idea of voluntary ethnicity: here too there are limits set by ethnohistory and political geography. As Billig puts it, "One can eat Chinese tomorrow and Turkish the day after; one can even dress in Chinese and Turkish styles. But *being* Chinese or Turkish are not commercially available options" (Billig 1995, 139, italics in original).

A second problem with social constructionism is its elitism. It is the ideas, strategies, and choices of elites—politicians, bureaucrats, officers, intellectuals, aristocrats, and business classes— that dominate the social constructionist portrayal of nationalism. Little attention is given to the popular basis of nationalism or to the involvement of other classes and strata in the creation or preservation of the nation.[9] While we can document many instances of elite manipulation of wider constituencies, it is equally important to analyze the ways in which popular outlooks, cultures, and traditions have influenced the perceptions and actions of elites. This was, as we saw, the burden of Francis Robinson's (1979) critique of Paul Brass in their debate about Islamic separatism in India.

Constructionists, moreover, are unable to grasp and credit the emotional depth of loyalties to historical nations and nationalisms. Even if the postmodernist characterization of contemporary humanity as "postemotional" and possessed of "pastiche personalities" were plausible, it remains the case that, only recently, millions of human beings were prepared to sacrifice their possessions and lives for "the defence of the motherland" (or fatherland), and in many parts of the world they still are. As George Mosse shows, through his analysis of mass volunteering for war and his concept of the civic religion and its liturgy, nationalism was singularly suited to tap into these needs and problems. Individuals were powerfully attracted to a nationalism that drew on past symbols exactly because it simultaneously answered to their changed needs and interests in a secular age (Mosse 1976, 1990).[10]

The final problem is the one that most concerns us here. In their concern to avoid imposing a "retrospective nationalism" on premodern communities and collective sentiments, modernists and constructionists have become blinkered by what John Peel has called a "blocking presentism," insisting that the needs and preoccupations of the present determine our view of the past. This means that nationalist memory becomes the focus of analysis rather than national history. What is decisive in their eyes is the view of the ethnic past entertained by present generations of the nation rather than the influence of that past on the national present. But as I shall argue, our view of the past is only partly shaped by present concerns; that past has the power also to shape present concerns by setting the cultural parameters and traditions for our present understandings, needs, and interests. For nations and their members, a long, documented, and distinctive history forms an essential part of the evidence, conditioning their understanding of the present and its data (Peel 1989; cf. Tonkin et al. 1989, introduction).

An Ethnosymbolic Account of Nations and Nationalism

The critique of social constructionism furnishes the basis for an alternative account of nations and nationalism and their historical locations and roles. It is essentially an ethnosymbolic account, and it seeks to link modern nations and nationalism with earlier collective cultural identities and sentiments. In what follows, I shall rehearse its main themes under seven headings: *la longue; durée; ethnie* and nation; ethnic myths, memories, and symbols, ethnic bases of nations, routes of nation formation; the role of nationalism; and finally, persistence and change of nations.

La Longue durée

Social constructionists begin their analyses of nations and nationalism from a modern, even contemporary standpoint or from a predicted future. In contrast, ethnosymbolists like John Armstrong, John Hutchinson, and myself stress the importance of treating the history of collective cultural identities and ideologies like nations and nationalism over long time spans. This is quite compatible with the evidence that nationalism is a modern ideological movement and that many nations are both recent and novel. But these modern nations are not created ex nihilo; they have premodern antecedents that require investigation in order to establish the basis on which they were formed. The relationship of the past, especially of the "ethnic past" or pasts, to the national present is crucial. There are three main ways in which the past may influence the national present:

1. *Recurrence*. If we recall our working definition of the concept of the nation as *a named human population occupying a historic territory or homeland and sharing common myths and memories; a mass, public culture; a single economy; and common rights and duties for all members*, then premodern collective cultural identities may approximate to this ideal type of the nation, at least for limited periods of time. For example, we might think of first-century-C.E. Jews and fifth-century Armenians as approximating to the ideal type of the nation. In this sense, the ideal type of the nation may be a recurrent phenomenon, even if its particular forms change in different epochs.[11]

2. *Continuity*. A second way in which the ethnic past may influence the national present is through established continuities. Here we are dealing with the possibility that the institutionalized elements and processes of some nations can be traced back through the generations before the onset of modernity. This too is a matter for empirical investigation on the basis of the ideal-type definition. In this sense, a number of Western European nations

can clearly demonstrate considerable continuities of institutional processes going back several centuries. This cannot be a simple either/or or before-and-after matter. The concept of the nation refers to processes that admit of degrees, such as territorialization, myth-making, memory formation, cultural unification, legal standardization and the like, that in their nature fluctuate and take new forms; and it must be a matter of judgment as to whether or when we can speak of a given collective cultural identity as a nation, and indeed when sufficient members and perhaps their neighbors deem that they constitute a nation.

3. *Appropriation*. A third way in which the past influences the present is through the tendency of later generations, especially of nationalists, to rediscover, authenticate, and appropriate aspects of what they assume is "their" ethnic past. This is, of course, an essential part of the ideology of nationalism itself, and it enables nationalists to give a convincing account and representation of the nation to their designated compatriots, as well as to outsiders. Finland provides a good example. There the nationalists, from Elias Lonnrot and Snellmann to Sibelius and Akseli Gallen-Kallela, sought to recover and portray Finland's heroic past, as recorded in the *Kalevala*. The world revealed by these Karelian ballads was represented as Finland's ancient history and treated as an authentic golden age. Only much later was a mythological interpretation of that past substituted for a historical understanding, though it lost none of its imaginative power for Finns. They still saw in the epic an allegory of their past, the image of the substratum of the recorded history of their country. This is in line with the cultural evolutionism of nationalism. In this view, the nation is multilayered, and the task of the nationalist historian and archaeologist is to recover each layer of the past and thereby trace the origins of the nation from its "rudimentary beginnings" through its early flowering in a golden age (or ages) to its periodic decline and its modern birth and renewal. In this way the myth receives apparent historical self-confirmation over the *longue durée*, and a rediscovered and authenticated past is "scientifically" appropriated for present national ends.[12]

Recurrence, continuity, appropriation: these are the ways in which the past is related to the present, and it may be an ancient and half-remembered past that must be recovered and authenticated. We can only begin to grasp the power exerted by such pasts if we extend our analysis of nations and nationalism well before the onset of modernity, to the collective cultural identities and communities of premodern epochs.

Ethnie *and Nation*

A second major theme is the distinction between the concepts of the ethnic community, or what the French term *ethnie,* and the nation. Here I define *ethnie* as *a named human population with myths of common ancestry, shared historical memories, one or more elements of shared culture, a link with a homeland, and a measure of solidarity, at least among the elites.* While *ethnies* share with nations the elements of common name, myth, and memory, their center of gravity is different: *ethnies* are defined largely by their ancestry myths and historical memories; nations are defined by the historic territory they occupy and by their mass, public cultures and common laws. A nation must possess its homeland; an *ethnie* need not—hence, the phenomenon of diaspora *ethnies.* In the case of the nation, a mass public culture encompasses all the members, whereas in the *ethnie* it may be confined to elite segments, for whom there may be a separate set of laws and a different type of education. For, as we saw, the concept of the nation includes both ethnic and civic elements: shared myths and memories but also common laws, a single economy, a historic territory, and a mass, public culture. In this way, the potential was there for nations to develop beyond single *ethnies* and incorporate and assimilate other *ethnies* or fragments thereof; or alternatively, to incorporate and accommodate diverse new *ethnies* in a polyethnic and multicultural nation (Krejci and Velimsky 1981, chap. 4; A. D. Smith 1986, chap. 2).

This separation of the concepts of *ethnie* and nation enables us to do justice to the insights of both modernism and perennialism. The modernists are surely justified in claiming that nationalism, as a doctrine and an ideological movement, is a modern phenomenon dating from the late eighteenth century and that many nations are also of fairly recent vintage. Equally, perennialists are right to point to the premodern continuities of at least *some* nations and to the recurrence, in different historical epochs, of a kind of collective cultural identity that may resemble the modern nation—resemble, but not be identical with the modern nation.

This is the case of that very common and ubiquitous type of collective cultural identity, the ethnic community, or *ethnie*. With the concept of *ethnie*, we can begin to do justice to the many collective cultural identities found in the ancient and medieval worlds, from Babylonians and Assyrians to Visigoths and Lombards; as well as to the many cultural communities that continue to exist alongside nations and within national states in the modern world (Connor 1994, chap. 2).

As for the modern nation, it may, from one angle, be regarded as an outgrowth and specialized political development of the *ethnie*; but from another angle, we may view it as a particular kind of territorial political community whose ideological ancestry can be traced to the classical Greek and Italian city-state. In the uneasy combination of these ethnocultural and ideological lines of descent lies the origin and much of the power of the modern concept of the nation, as well of its various formulations.

Ethnic Myths, Memories, and Symbols

As the name implies, ethnosymbolism regards the central components of ethnic and national phenomena as both sociocultural and symbolic, rather than demographic or political. Apart from various symbols, like language, dress, emblems, rituals, and artifacts, these elements consist in memories, myths, values, and traditions and in the institutionalized practices that derive from them. These are the elements that John Armstrong emphasized in his concept of ethnic "myth-symbol complexes." Following Fredrik Barth, Armstrong argued that distinctive clusters of these symbolic components mark out and guard the boundaries of *ethnies*. Such symbolic clusters are both subjective, in their reference to individual perceptions and beliefs, and objective because their patterning produces a structure of social relations and cultural institutions that persist across the generations, independent of any individual beliefs and perceptions (Barth 1969, introduction; Armstrong 1982, chap. 1).

Of particular importance are myths, symbols, and memories of ethnic origins, election, homeland, and the golden age. The historical record is replete with examples of myths of origin, from those of ancient Sumer, Israel, and Rome to the Russian myth of Rurik and his Varangians, the Swiss Oath of the Rütli, the Turkish myth of Oguz Khan, and the Aztec myth of Tenochtitlan (see Kushner

1976; Pipes 1977; Kreis 1991; Gutierrez 1999). Along with shared memories, these ancestry myths define the distinctive character of specific *ethnies*. The myth of being ancestrally related, even if it is purely fictive and ideological in character, endows the members of a community with a powerful sense of belonging (Tudor 1972; A. D. Smith 1984; Connor 1994, chap. 8; cf. Hosking and Schöpflin 1997).

Equally widespread and even more potent have been ethnic myths of divine election, the belief that certain peoples have been entrusted by the deity with a sacred mission on earth, in some cases through a holy covenant. The prototype of covenantal election myths is ancient Israel, enjoined to be a holy people and a kingdom of priests by obeying the Torah at all times. These myths are conditional: they make election and salvation dependent on fulfillment of a strict ritual and moral code. Such myths could be found among Protestant communities like those of the early American settlers, the Afrikaners, and the Ulster Scots. There is also a wide variety of less stringent, missionary myths of chosenness, and they can be found among a host of peoples in the monotheistic traditions, such as Armenians; Byzantine Orthodox Greeks; Orthodox Russians; Muslim Arabs; Shi'ite Persians; Catholic Poles, Irish, French, and Catalans; and Protestant English, Dutch, and Welsh. Their role in the formation of national identities requires further study (Sherrard 1959; O'Brien 1988; Akenson 1992; Cauthen 1997).

If myths of ethnic election provide powerful cultural resources for ethnic persistence and mobilization, memories of ancestral homelands and sacred territories set limits to and provide direction for ethnic and later national goals. In the case of island peoples like the Japanese and English or mountain peoples like the Swiss, the link between "ethnoscapes" and ancestral memory is fairly clear. But even in more ambiguous cases, memories of battles, heroes, and sages may sanctify ancestral homelands and direct collective energies toward their recovery or retention; the battles of the Boyne, Kosovo-Polje, Avarayr, and Karbala and the fall of Jerusalem all attest to the continuing power of ancient territorial memories. (See Hooson 1994; A. D. Smith 1997b; Kaufmann and Zimmer 1998.)

Similarly, memories of political, religious, economic, and artistic "golden ages" may continue to inspire later generations of that *ethnie* and become the canon of authenticity and creativity for latter-day nationalists. That was how Mexican intellectuals at the turn of the century came to view the glories of Teotihuacan and the later Aztec empire; how Greek intellectuals looked back to the golden age of Pericles; how some Egyptian nationalists took pride in their pharaonic past; and how some modern Indians began to rediscover the age of the post-Vedic classical city-states; and Russian nationalists harked back to legendary golden ages in Kievan Rus and tribal Russia. (See McCulley 1966; Campbell and Sherrard 1968, chap. 1; Gershoni and Jankowski 1987, chap. 7; Florescano 1993; A. D. Smith 1997a; Gutierrez 1999.)[13]

Such memories of territory, heroes, and golden ages form important elements of what we may term the *ethnohistory* of each *ethnie*, its own self-understanding as these events have been remembered and handed down by successive generations of the community. They are all the more powerful in scope and intensity when they are linked to particular institutions like the law, the church, the state, or the schools, as John Breuilly (1996a) has forcefully reminded us. But they are also embedded in languages and customs, rituals and mores, as well as in the arts and crafts, music and dances, of ethnic communities, all of which make up the ethnohistory of culture communities.

Such ethnic memories are, of course, partial, changing, and often contested. There is usually more than one "ethnic past," and different interpretations may generate acute conflicts. A classic example is the rival interpretations of key episodes of the French past, such as the Revolution and Napoleon, as the essays in Pierre Nora's *Lieux de Memoire* (1984, 1986) and Robert Gildea's (1994) analysis suggest. Similar conflicts attended the interpretation of the role of Joan of Arc, as Ingres's painting *St. Joan at the Coronation of Charles VII* (1854) suggests—she is depicted as a pure and militant warrior for faith and country—responding to the new religious medievalism sweeping France in the Second Empire. These rival interpretations and conflicts, whether in France or Sri Lanka, Yugoslavia or Israel, may serve to uphold the cultural parameters of the *ethnie* or the nation, for they take place within a definite set of cultural presuppositions and taken-for-granted historical assumptions. Moreover, the fact that some *ethnies* can boast a long, well-documented ethnohistory, while others cannot, encourages keen cultural competition, thereby reinforcing the differences in national profiles (Schöpflin 1980; Rosenblum 1985; Kapferer 1988; van der Veer 1994; Ram 1998).

Ethnic Bases of Nations

With the conceptual tools noted above, we can begin to interpret the historical record of collective cultural identities and sentiments as predominantly one in which *ethnies* flourished alongside other collectivities in the ancient and medieval epochs of empires, city-states, and kingdoms and as one where both *ethnies* and nations can be found side by side or in superordinate and subordinate positions in the modern epoch of national states. But this is only a first approximation. Such a vast overgeneralization conceals from view the many complexities of collective identity and sentiment in all periods. Thus, in several cases we find elements of nationhood stretching back to the late medieval period—in a few cases, even into the ancient world—as well as all kinds of *ethnie* (ethnolinguistic, ethnoreligious, and ethnopolitical) in every stage of organization, self-consciousness, and self-assertion.[14]

If this view forms a realistic point of departure for analysis, then the modernists' simplistic periodization of the historical role of nations and nationalism must be rethought. We can still agree that nations, like nationalisms, are for the most part relatively recent, that most nations emerged after the late eighteenth century. This is particularly true if, with Walker Connor, we accept the idea that nations are mass territorial phenomena or, with Breuilly, we hold that mass citizenship is essential to the very idea of the nation. Even if we do not, even if we concede that there may be elite or middle-class nations, with or without a wider citizenship, the number of the nations that can be shown to have flourished prior to the eighteenth century is limited. And if we go back beyond the sixteenth century, the number is still smaller. (See A. D. Smith 1994; Connor 1994, chap. 9.)

But this does not entail acceptance of the modernists' further contention that nations are the products of modernity or of modernization. Quite apart from the few but important cases that antedated even an elastic version of the concepts of modernity and modernization, we cannot derive the identity, the location, or even the character of the units that we term nations from the processes of modernization *tout court*. We must go further back and look at the premodern social and cultural antecedents and contexts of these emergent nations to explain why these and not other communities and territories became nations and why they emerged where they did. Modernists may provide more or less convincing answers to the questions "Why is the nation?" and "When is the nation?" But they have much less to tell us in answer to such questions as "Who is the nation?" and "Where is the nation?" For answers to such questions, we must turn to the ethnosymbolists.

What does this mean for the three cultural communities that lay claim to a long history of nationhood—the Persians, Jews, and Greeks? Insofar as they now constitute "national states," they are also clearly *modern* nations; but the contents of their national identities retain distinctive earlier and premodern ethnosymbolic elements—myths, memories, values, and traditions—that inspire and legitimate their present claims to land and statehood. In earlier periods such elements clustered to form Persian, Jewish, and Greek *ethnies*, whether they were politically united or divided, whether they occupied a homeland or were dispersed; and collective memories of these ancient *ethnies*, transmitted in texts, artifacts, and institutions, provided specific models for subsequent claims to nationhood, especially in times of crisis.

This is not to say that every emergent nation is formed through a specific ethnic model, much less that there is a one-to-one relationship between each modern nation and "its" antecedent *ethnie*. Things are never so straightforward. Even the strongest contemporary nations—those with the most developed sense of a distinct national identity and powerful myth of descent—can point to diverse ethnic origins and can be shown to have incorporated elements from several *ethnies* over a long period of time. The English, for example, incorporated ethnic and cultural elements from Celtic tribes, Roman conquerors, Anglo-Saxons, Danes, and Normans, not to mention much later immigrant waves of Huguenots, Jews, Poles, Cypriots, Afro-Caribbeans, and Asians. The same is true of other "strong" national identities, like the French, the Spanish, and the Dutch. At the same time, a rough correspondence of dominant *ethnie* and subsequent nation has lent credence to the myths and memories of nationhood imparted to successive generations; and the model of the earlier *ethnie* continues to resonate through its traditions, memories, and symbols. (See

Hastings 1997, chap. 8; Poliakov 1974; MacDougall 1982; Colley 1992.)

Routes of Nation Formation

How, then, may we trace the genealogies and the formation of modern nations?

An important assumption of an ethnosymbolic approach is the need to analyze the rise of nations in terms of antecedent ethnic ties and popular formations. Kingdoms tended to be formed around certain "ethnic cores"—dominant populations united by presumed ties of common descent and vernacular culture, which, in certain cases, gradually expanded to incorporate outlying regions and their *ethnies* as well as lower classes—as occurred with the early nations in the West, such as the English, French, Castilians, and Swedes (Tilly 1975, introduction; A. D. Smith 1986, chap. 6).[15]

Within this framework, various patterns of nation formation can be traced. For John Armstrong, a variety of factors over the *longue durée* have influenced the emergence of nations, including differences in nomadic and sedentary lifestyles, the influence of great religious civilizations like Christianity and Islam, the impact of imperial administrations and *mythomoteurs* (constitutive political myths), different patterns of ecclesiastical organization, and, at the lowest level, the incidence of language "fault lines" and of particular European languages. For John Hutchinson, nations emerge through an oscillation and interplay between cultural, regenerative kinds of nationalism and state-oriented political movements. One should add that the processes by which nations are formed are not linear, determinate, nor irreversible; there is considerable variation and indeed uncertainty in many cases. (See Eisenstadt 1965; Armstrong 1982; Hutchinson 1987, chap. 1 and 1994, chap. 2.)

For myself, the starting point of the process is the type of *ethnie*, though that influence may be modified by the epoch in which the process takes place. Here I distinguish three kinds of *ethnie*: the "lateral" or aristocratic; the "vertical" or demotic; and the "fragmentary" or immigrant. The last are, in fact, part-*ethnies*, whose members have migrated from their community to form a new colony, for economic, religious, or political reasons; and over time such ethnic fragments may become estranged from their *ethnie* and form a new nation, as has been the case with the pioneering immigrant nations of America, Canada, South Africa, and Australia (Tuveson 1968; Hutchinson 1994, chap. 6).

The other two patterns of nation formation comprise the vast majority of cases. Lateral, or aristocratic, *ethnies* tend to be extensive, with ragged boundaries and little social depth; they rarely resort to cultural penetration of "the people," whom they may fail to recognize as "theirs," as occurred in Eastern Europe. Vertical, or demotic, *ethnies*, on the other hand, are intensive, with relatively compact boundaries, high barriers to entry, and deep, albeit at times uneven, cultural penetration of all classes. In the first case, the route to modern nationhood proceeds through the establishment by the nobles of a strong, centralized state and through the *bureaucratic incorporation* of outlying regions and lower strata by that state and its aristocratic culture. This was the pattern found in Western Europe and repeated, with varying success, by the ex-colonial "state nations" of Asia and sub-Saharan Africa. In the second case, an indigenous intelligentsia rediscovers, authenticates, and appropriates for political use the vernacular cultures of the lower strata and through the *vernacular mobilization* of these strata attempts to rouse them to political action so as to create ethnic nations—a pattern common in Eastern Europe and the Middle East (A. D. Smith 1989 and 1991, chap. 5).[16]

The Role of Nationalism

As these last remarks suggest, the routes of nation formation are not explicable wholly in terms of antecedent structures and processes. They involve vital elements of conscious agency—elite choices, popular responses, and ideological motivations. Of the last, the most important has been the modern ideology of nationalism itself. The basic tenets of this ideology may be summarized as follows:

1. The world is divided into nations, each possessing a distinctive character, history, and destiny.
2. Political power resides solely in the nation, and loyalty to the nation overrides all other loyalties.
3. To be free, human beings must identify with a nation.

4. To be authentic, nations must have maximum autonomy.

5. World peace and justice can be built only on a society of autonomous nations.

Such a doctrine does not pretend to supply a complete political program but rather a basic framework for different programs. It holds up three ideals that all political programs must realize: national autonomy, national unity, and national identity. These, the nationalist argues, are the sine qua non of a free society and of a peaceful and just international order, and thereby nationalism provides a blueprint for the aspirations and liberation of all would-be nations (A. D. Smith 1991, 74).[17]

The power of nationalism is not only a matter of ideology. Perhaps even more potent than nationalist principles have been national symbols. These give concrete meaning and visibility to the abstractions of nationalism. The representations and images of the nation exert a profound influence over large numbers of people, exactly because they can be very widely disseminated by the media. In each of these media, specific images of the nation and its liberation, its heroic past, and its glorious future can be created and purveyed, so that the nation ceases to be the abstract property of intellectuals and becomes the immemorial imagined community of all those designated as its members and citizens. Through opera, music, drama, novels, films, and television, artists have continually conveyed the power and tangibility of their nations through a dramatic and artistically authentic re-creation of their heroic pasts. Throughout Europe and beyond, this "historical mobility" and "archaeological verisimilitude" became increasingly popular: in paintings by Delaroche in France, Surikov and Vasnetsov in Russia, and Diego Rivera and Orozco in Mexico, we see this desire to invest the national past with drama, grandeur, and period authenticity. Yet even when they depicted contemporary national dramas in modern dress, as in Benjamin West's graphic yet stylized *Death of General Wolfe* (1770) and David's much more immediate and tangible *Marat Assassiné* (1793), artists drew on sentiments and compositions derived from earlier Christian and classical motifs. (See Honour 1968, chap. 3; A. D. Smith 1993.)

This tangibility is also present in the many festivals and ceremonies celebrating the nation and commemorating its fallen soldiers and the "glorious dead." Nationalism, as a self-reflexive ideology of community, preaches the need for liberty, fraternity, and solidarity, particularly in suffering; and nowhere are these sentiments and bonds more palpably expressed than in the common grief and collective piety for the sacrifice of war heroes who fell in defense of the fatherland or motherland. These national festivals, commemorations, and monuments form the major focus of the late George Mosse's oeuvre. Mosse argued that nationalism should be regarded as a popular form of civic religion, with a specific liturgy and rites appropriate to a secular, political religion of the masses. He dated the rise of such orchestrated and choreographed mass civic religions from the great fêtes of the French Revolution and traced their course in Western Europe, especially in Germany, culminating in the fascist rallies and commemorations. He also detailed the development of tombs, cemeteries, and monuments to the heroic dead, from the Pantheon (1757–91) to the cemeteries of the First World War. Where Mosse's account departs from classic modernism is not only in its emphasis on the mass symbolic and cultural elements of the nation but in its analysis of the persistence and revival of premodern Christian and classical motifs and imagery in the liturgy and symbolism of nationalism. Two striking examples in Britain are the ceremonies held on Remembrance Sunday at the Cenotaph (1919) in Whitehall and Stanley Spencer's more private vision of the soldiers' resurrection in the First World War, in the Sandham Chapel (1928–32) at Burghclere. Once again, this suggests the historical embeddedness of nationalist imagery in earlier religious and ethnic symbolisms and, given the large number of ethnic nationalisms in the contemporary world, the deep-rooted power of the forces for both national liberation and ethnic exclusion (Mosse 1976, 1990, 1994).[18]

Persistence and Change of Nations

But this also means that we have not yet entered a postnational epoch. It is true that national identities in advanced Western societies are undergoing significant transformations consequent on the loss of empire and the large-scale immigration of culturally different peoples. This is reflected in the many debates in the media about interpretations of national identity, the import and teaching of national histories, and the rival visions and projects for national destinies, as well as the many human rights afforded to immigrant nonnationals that are organized by the national states but originate with international or regional (European) treaties and conventions. But none of this implies the disintegration of nations and the fading away of national identities, only their transformation by global forces (Soysal 1994; Billig 1995, chap. 6).

Contrary to the prognoses of constructionists and other postmodernists, ethnosymbolic approaches argue that we are unlikely to realize the supersession of nationalism or the transcendence of nations for many decades to come. They do not base their predictions only on the vivid and widespread evidence of contemporary surges of nationalisms in various parts of the globe nor only on the importance that many people, even in the most developed parts of the world, still attach to their national identities. Both of these phenomena, ethnosymbolists would claim, derive from the preexisting symbols and cultural ties and sentiments in which nations are embedded. It is therefore a grave error to commence analyses of nations and nationalism from the nineteenth century or later. Not only is such a standpoint historically shallow; it fails to appreciate the immense cultural networks and resources on which modern nations draw and that make the nation so much more tangible and salient than the larger regional or global identities mooted by postnationalists.

This is why even such powerful political projects as the European Union find it so difficult to transcend and subsume the nations of Europe. Not only do such regional projects lack unifying myths, memories, and symbols, but those that Europe might be tempted to draw on are either divisive and unacceptable, like Catholic Christendom or the Holy Roman Empire, or freighted with bitter memories, like the European traditions of revolution or the world wars.[19]

Outside Europe, meanwhile, the fires of ethnic nationalism continue to burn, providing the international community with its bloodiest and most intractable problems. Once again, these national aspirations are fed by preexisting ethnic traditions, symbols, myths, and memories in each region and state. Achinese and Moro, Karens and Tamils, Kashmiris and Sikhs, Palestinians, Kurds, Somalis, and Oromo, to name just a few of the many ethnic or ethnically oriented conflicts in Asia and Africa, draw on often bitter histories of cultural difference and collective memories; while in Europe itself, the many cultural conflicts involving Muslims, Gypsies, and Afro-Caribbeans are exceeded in intensity and scope only by the savage wars waged in the former Yugoslavia. In the aftermath of the cold war we are witnessing once again the territorialization of memory, the politicization of chosenness, and the reappropriation of a heroic past—in other words, the basic processes underlying nation formation and the reemergence of nationalism. It is still nationalist high noon, and the owl of Minerva has not stirred (see Suny 1993b).

Conclusion

Taken together, these themes and the ethnosymbolic approach from which they spring have the potential to clarify many of the debates surrounding ethnicity and nationalism and to provide a deeper approach to the problem of the role of nations and nationalism in history. The major debates between primordialists, perennialists, and modernists fall into place if we adopt the distinction between *ethnie* and nation and employ a methodology of *la longue durée* to reveal the complex relations of past, present, and future and the place of *ethnies* and nations within them. It then becomes possible to avoid a retrospective nationalism while doing justice to the widespread presence and significance of collective cultural identities in premodern epochs. Ethnosymbolic approaches point to ways in which these earlier collective cultural identities may be related to modern nations while allowing for historical discontinuities between them and for the possibility of novel combinations of ethnic categories and communities in the making of recent nations.

Similarly, an emphasis on symbolic and cultural components enables us to dispense with biological references while addressing the fundamental problem of the emotional power and hold of nationalism and its capacity for inspiring mass devotion and self-sacrifice, an issue that modernists have tended to leave for an unsatisfactory and misleading cultural primordialism to pick up. The importance of symbolic and cultural issues in ethnic conflicts and national aspirations is one that requires as much attention as the material and political aspects.

Ethnosymbolic approaches also are helpful in directing our attention away from an exclusive concern with elites and their strategies, for they seek to go beyond the "top-down" approaches of modernism in order to bring the popular, emotional, and moral dimensions of national identity back into focus. But they do so in a manner that avoids the reifying tendencies of primordialism and the politically dangerous ideas of organic nationalism. At the same time, ethnosymbolic analysis helps us to avoid seeing modern nationalisms in terms of simplistic dichotomies like "civic" and "ethnic"; by adopting a more nuanced analysis, it enables us to recognize the great variety of historical and symbolic components of particular nationalisms at specific historical junctures.

Most of all perhaps, an ethnosymbolic approach can help us to understand both the durability and the transformations of ethnicity in history and the continuing power and persistence of nations and nationalism at the start of the third millennium. This is because it directs our gaze to the inner worlds of the *ethnie* and the nation. By relating nations and nationalism to prior ethnic ties and sentiments, it becomes possible to grasp the hold that particular nations still possess over so many individuals despite all the pressures of a global modernity to undermine the sense of the past and detach it from the immediate present and future. An ethnosymbolic approach invites the analyst to enter the inner worlds of ethnicity and nationalism—their memories, myths, traditions, and symbols—and to study the changes they undergo as well as the symbolic components that endure. But it also encourages the detachment necessary to enable the scholar both to explain and to evaluate those worlds, and it does so by narrating a particular kind of history of ethnic and national phenomena—one that, while setting out from the ethnohistories of the participants, seeks to locate and explain them within a broad sociological framework and long historical time span. The upshot of this examination of histories of the nation has been to show that we can best grasp the character, role, and persistence of the nation in history if we relate it to the symbolic components and ethnic models of earlier collective cultural identities.

Notes

Foreword

1. M. Stern, "H. H. Ben-Sasson: In Memoriam," *Zion* 54 (1989): 146. (Hebrew)
2. Introduction, *History of the Jewish People*, ed. H. H. Ben-Sasson, 3 vols. (Tel Aviv, 1969), 1: xv–xvi. (Hebrew)
3. Ibid., xvi, xix.
4. M. Stern, "The Zealots and the Sicarii: Branches of a National Liberation Movement," *Cathedra* 1 (1976): 52–55. (Hebrew)
5. A. D. Smith, *Nationalism and Modernism: A Critical Survey of Recent Theories of Nations and Nationalism* (London and New York, 1998), 226.
6. A. D. Smith, *National Identity* (Harmondsworth, U.K., 1991); idem, "Chosen Peoples: Why Ethnic Groups Survive," *Ethnic and Racial Studies* 15 (1992): 436–56; idem, *Nationalism and Modernism*, 192.
7. Smith, *Nationalism and Modernism*, 195.
8. Ibid., 226.
9. Ibid., 117–42.
10. Ibid., 225.

Introduction (pp. 2–3)

1. For some earlier analyses of historiographical debates, see the essays in Tipton (1972). For some more recent debates, see Forde, Johnson, and Murray (1995). I have briefly outlined some historians' accounts of nations and nationalism in A. D. Smith (1992b).
2. There is a possible fifth paradigm, the postmodernist, in the making, as it were. But in practice it refers to a rather loose and inchoate set of approaches and can hardly be termed a fully fledged paradigm, since these varied approaches accept the basic modernist understandings, which they then seek to go beyond. (See Bhabha 1990; A. D. Smith 1998, chap. 9.)
3. There are, of course, as many definitions of these key terms as there are scholars and interpretations. For other definitions, see Snyder (1954), Deutsch (1966, chap. 1), and Connor (1994, chap. 4).

1. Voluntarism and the Organic Nature (pp. 5–25)

1. There are several meanings for the term *primordial*. Here I follow that suggested by Clifford Geertz (1973; see below) rather than that of Eliade (1958).

2. For an incisive application of sociobiology to ethnic groups and nations, see van den Berghe (1978, 1995). For critiques, see V. Reynolds (1980) and A. D. Smith (1998, 147–51).

3. Subsequent analysis has generally reinforced the distinction between the two kinds of nationalism, recast as either voluntarist and organic (the ideological distinction, with which I am concerned here) or as territorial and ethnic (the sociological distinction that imperfectly parallels the ideological). See the critiques of Kohn's dichotomy in A. D. Smith (1983, chap. 8) and in Hutchinson (1987, chap. 1).

4. Not to mention the writings of Burke, Zimmerman, and Moser. The idea of the nation also had been popularized in France by the *parlements* in their struggle with the Crown; on which, see Palmer (1940) and Baker (1988, 228–35).

5. Rousseau was even more influenced by the examples of civic solidarity afforded by the city-states of classical antiquity; by his example, he gave a powerful impetus to the growing tide of neoclassicism in literature and the arts; on which, see Leith (1965) and Rosenblum (1967).

6. Since the work of Hans Kohn (1965, 1967b), there has been no full-scale study of rival conceptions of the nation in Europe in this period; but see the interesting analyses in Llobera (1994, part 3) and Sluga (1998).

7. Thus, for Michelet, a single nation, France, was the natural leader of the movement to realize the universal Rousseauian vision of a return to nature in an era of liberty and fraternity. Similar tensions could be found in the work of nationalist historians from Karamzin to Palacky and Treitschke; see Kohn (1960, 1961, and [1944] 1967a, chaps. 5–8).

8. According to Thom (1990), Renan was greatly influenced by the work of Thierry and Fustel de Coulanges, whose anti-Germanist interpretation of French origins forced Renan to reconsider and soften his Germanist (Frankish) approach.

9. There is a rapidly growing literature on liberalism and nationalism and the possibility of a "liberal nationalism"; see especially Tamir (1993), Gutmann (1994), Miller (1995), and Kymlicka (1995).

10. Marx and Engels tended to accept a Herderian definition of the nation (as a people united by language and natural sympathies), but Engels also espoused a Hegelian theory of "historyless peoples," arguing that peoples who in the past had been unable to build states would be unable to do so in the future and were therefore destined to become so many "ethnographic monuments." See Davis (1967) and Connor (1984).

11. There is a huge literature on the "ethnic revival" in the West and (after 1989) in the East; see especially Esman (1977), A. D. Smith (1981), Tiryakian and Rogowski (1985), Suny (1993b), Bremmer and Taras (1993), and my general interpretation in A. D. Smith (1996b).

12. Miller's book sparked a lively debate in the special symposium in *Nations and Nationalism*; see O'Leary (1996).

13. While there is a clear normative distinction, I am not persuaded of any substantive difference between patriotism and nationalism. But see Doob (1964) and the rigorous distinction drawn in terms of ethnicity (ethnonationalism) and territorial polity (patriotism) by Connor (1994). But I do not think we can demonstrate systematic differences in sentiments and subsequent actions.

14. On the Catholic foundations of the medieval French kingdom, see Armstrong (1982, 154–59) and Beaune (1985).

15. For the idea of Scotland as a case of a "civic nation," with a purely civic nationalism, see Ichijo (1998); see also McCrone (1998, chap. 2).

16. Neither Geertz nor Shils uses the term *primordialism*; the term is used by the critics of this position (or indeed of anything resembling it). See the debate in *Ethnic and Racial Studies* between Eller and Coughlan (1993) and Grosby (1994); see also Wilmsen and McAllister (1996, introduction).

17. Fishman attacks the three roadblocks to a deeper understanding of ethnicity and nationalism. These are (1) civility, the Western liberal assumptions held by Lord Acton and John Stuart Mill that history necessarily progressed from the politics of group loyalties to those of individual liberty and that Western civility was threatened by the group passions of ethnic nationalism; (2) radicalism, the Marxist assumption that ethnicity is at best a secondary cultural diversion from the evils of industrial capitalism, at worst a specious fabrication of the bourgeoisie to divide the proletariat; and (3) modernity, the sociologists' assumption that the processes of modernization would cause ethnic distinctions to diminish and eventually to disappear as a result of technological homogenization. Only by overcoming these roadblocks can we hope to attain a more sympathetic understanding of unmobilized ethnicity, free of bias and mechanical rationalism (Fishman 1980, 69–99).

18. For further theoretical statements of aspects of cultural primordialism, see Shils (1995) and Grosby (1995). For a fuller discussion, see A. D. Smith (1998, chap. 7).

2. The Nation: Modern or Perennial? (pp. 27–50)

1. On this earlier perennialism, which is not to be confused with the primordialism discussed above, as well as the critique mounted by modernism, see A. D. Smith (1998, chap. 1).

2. For overviews of these pioneers of the study of nationalism, see Snyder (1954) and A. D. Smith (1983, chaps. 8–9).

3. For these earlier debates, and some empirical cases, see the essays in Tipton (1972); cf. also Guenée (1985).

4. For fuller discussions of Kedourie's approach and account of nationalism, see A. D. Smith (1983, chaps. 1, 2; 1998, chap. 5). For the background to Elie Kedourie's outlook, see the illuminating essays in S. Kedourie (1998). Despite his philosophical debt to Oakeshott, Kedourie is, in many ways, the political heir of Lord Acton, though his attitude toward nationalism is influenced both by his Jewish faith and his own early experiences in an (increasingly) virulently nationalist Baghdad.

5. For fuller discussions of Ernest Gellner's theory, see A. D. Smith (1983, chap. 6; 1998, chap. 2) and the essays in J. Hall (1998).

6. Breuilly's definition of nationalist doctrine is decidedly particularist; he refuses to admit any universalist element in the nationalist outlook. While this holds for many nationalists, even the most extreme know that they must operate in a world of nations and accordingly acknowledge a plural world of sovereign nations. The word *nation* describes both an attribute and a relationship, and the doctrine of nationalism always assumes a polycentric political environment. This is one of the main differences between the modern doctrine of nationalism and earlier ethnicism, though even the Greeks and Jews knew that they must deal with a world of other peoples. (See E. Hall 1992.)

7. In this, Breuilly agrees with Leonard Thompson's (1985) account; cf. also the penetrating analysis of Akenson (1992).

8. See the parallel account by Hughes (1988). Greater attention is given to language and discursive networks in Bruford (1965) and Barnard (1965, introduction). For Ulrich von Hutten and the German Renaissance humanists, see Kohn ([1944] 1967a, 133–46).

9. For Hegel's theory of "historyless peoples," see Rosdolsky (1964). Hobsbawm (1990, 63–67) oscillates between a genetic meaning of ethnicity and a cultural one and is thereby able to portray ethnicity as ambiguous and shifting.

10. Gellner's view came out in the debate with me at Warwick University, his last public appearance before his untimely death, when he cited the case of Israel as a purely modern nation forging a "high culture" and thereby enabled to meet the challenges of the modern world. In such a society, the culture of the past is irrelevant, if not an impediment; see A. D. Smith (1996a).

11. These are what Charles Tilly called "nations of design." Such deliberately and often swiftly created nations are usually the outcome of treaties consequent upon periods of protracted warfare, like the Napoleonic wars and the First World War. Such nations include many in Eastern Europe and Asia, for example, the Czechs and Slovaks, Rumanians, Serbs, Croats, Albanians, Ukrainians, Estonians, Azeris, Kurds, Syrians, Pakistanis, Malaysians, and Indonesians. See Tilly (1975, conclusion) and Seton-Watson (1977, chaps. 3–4).

12. Such myths generally traced the royal house to Trojan or biblical (Noah) origins and were recorded by writers like Isidore of Seville, Orderic Vitalis, and Geoffrey of Monmouth, often on behalf of the ruling dynasty. Though we should not confuse these myths of origin with their modern

nationalist counterparts, they performed many of the same functions; see Davis (1976) and Reynolds (1983).

13. That was the finding of Hans Kohn in one of his early studies (1940). More generally, see the work of Marcu (1976) and Guenée (1985).

14. According to Hastings (1997, chap. 6), nations formed subsequently outside the Christian orbit were directly or indirectly stimulated by Christian nationalisms (or by nationalisms that emerged in the non-European world under Christian influence), as in sub-Saharan Africa and South Asia.

15. It may therefore be misleading to search for a single temporal origin of the nation, particularly without a clear definition of the concept. All we can say is that in a certain period, after careful definition of terms, we may legitimately speak of an English or Irish nation, because the various processes that help to forge communities have ensured that they approximate the ideal type of the nation. On this, see A. D. Smith (1994).

16. For a penetrating and balanced assessment of the merits and limitations of rival modernist and ethnosymbolic approaches and their uses for Asian communities and nationalisms, see Tonnesson and Antlov (1996, introduction).

17. Here Hastings appears to confuse the nation with the state. We saw how, after the dissolution of their sovereign state and the partition of the territory, the Poles sought advice from Rousseau, who counseled them on the vital importance of preserving and cultivating their national identity through a program of public education and commemorative festivals. For Weber (1947), too, state and nation were to be carefully distinguished, with the implication that the German nation, for example, predated its expression in a sovereign state. Hastings concedes that the Jews continued as a nation after the fall of Jerusalem, but he also claims that they had lost their "model of nationhood" (Hastings 1997, 186–87). Is there, then, a difference between being a nation and possessing nationhood?

18. For Grosby (1997), agreeing here with Finley, ancient Greece lacked the attributes of nationhood: a single, bounded land; a single god above the pantheon; a common law of the land; and a single cult center (presumably, Delphi failed to qualify). It also lacked a single economy; but it could boast a single public culture, including Hellenic games; an Olympian pantheon; Greek colonies; and a Greek family of languages, as well as common Homeric myths and memories.

19. Nevertheless, there were clear divisions between eastern, western, and northern Iran, often with rival regional dynasties, between the fall of the Sassanids and the rise of the Safavids. See Saunders (1978).

20. On the unities and divisions of Egypt from the Old Kingdom to the late Saite period, see Trigger et al. (1983); and for other ancient peoples in the Near East, see Wiseman (1973).

21. Interestingly, for Grosby, the fiction of a blood tie is secondary; it derives in large part from a bounded, translocal territory. Grosby is unclear why this should be so; he appears to think it is the result of the

primordial, life-sustaining character of the land. I am not so sure. In the case of ancient Israel, the relationship appears to be reversed: the kingdom and land appear to succeed and to be named after the children of Israel and their eponymous patriarch. In any case, it is difficult to prove a one-way causal relationship, and at this point, Grosby seems to forsake causal historical analysis for a more general sociological speculation.

22. But the question remains: can we designate Jewish ethnic sentiments and actions in this period as nationalist without anachronism? Even the Zealots fought not for a secular political nation of Israel but for the independence of the Lord's heritage—the land of Israel and its resources—from Roman rule and oppression; in other words, for a purely religious conception. But, per contra, it can be argued that for Jews in this and much later periods there was and there could be no distinction between a "faith community" and a nation nor indeed between religion and politics. Such a distinction would be meaningless. Might it then be necessary to argue that such a distinction is an essential condition of the rise of nationalism and its ideal of an independent nation? Or does this formulation betray too modernist and secular a reading of the concept of nationalism? On the idea of a faith community, see Klausner (1960).

23. The bulk of Mendels's subsequent analysis is devoted to showing the ways in which these political symbols influenced the beliefs and actions of not only the Jews of Palestine in this period but of all the Hellenistic peoples and kingdoms. Preeminent among these beliefs and actions were those of a nationalist character. For the Jews, of course, this culminated in the massive Jewish support given to the Zealots in 66 C.E. against the vehement opposition of the many non-Jews and Roman supporters in first-century Palestine. The disturbing presence of so many non-Jews in Palestine, from Herod's time, had created a large cultural gap or "schizophrenia" between Jews and non-Jews, as well as within Jewish society; this proved to be, as Josephus claimed, the major cause of the Jewish War of 66–73 C.E.; and it explains why, in the Near East, only the Jews revolted on such a scale (Mendels 1992, 356–58).

24. They went on to claim that this people was, in essence, the same nation that had entered the land of Canaan under Joshua, been exiled twice from the promised land, and endured nearly two thousand years of exile; now, once again, it was resuming its national destiny in its own land. They reasoned that, despite all the internal social and cultural differentiation of Jewish communities worldwide, only such a unitary conception of Jewish nationality could make sense of present-day Jewish realities. (See Dinur 1969.)

25. In a later article, Armstrong (1992) speaks of a distinction between nations that arose before 1800 and those that emerged after that date, the latter being assisted by the ideology of nationalism. But, rather like Hastings, he does not attribute much significance to the ideology of nationalism, except perhaps as a legitimating catalyst for national self-determination.

3. *Social Construction and Ethnic Genealogy (pp. 53–75)*

1. John Peel (1989) speaks of the "cultural work" of creating a pan-Yoruba *ethnie* out of the many Yoruba-speaking regions and chieftainships, by a Yoruba intelligentsia in the late nineteenth century.

2. Here Hobsbawm shifts from analysis of the "nation" to speaking about the "territorial state." Why should it follow that, because the state is modern, the nation too must be recent and novel? Presumably, for Hobsbawm, because states (and nationalism) created the nation. But this is exactly what is so often in dispute. See the criticisms in Hastings (1997, chap. 1) and A. D. Smith (1998, chaps. 4, 6).

3. There is a large and growing literature on collective memory and its relationship with national identity, notably the work of Mosse (1990, 1994), Pierre Nora and his colleagues (Nora 1984, 1986), and Jan Assmann (1997); see also Gillis (1994), Zerubavel (1995), and Ram (1998).

4. For the Swiss foundation myth and early history of the Swiss Eidgenossenschaft, see Im Hof (1991); the chronicles of Tschudi and others were based on the fifteenth-century White Book of Sarnen, containing the earliest reference to William Tell and his exploits. See also Kohn (1957).

5. Though it expired as a political policy in the disaster of 1922, the Megale Idea still reverberates, and in cultural terms it resonates in the continuing importance of Greek Orthodoxy in defining "Greekness" and in the emotional link with Byzantium and Constantinople. (See Sherrard 1959.)

6. While the Israeli "new historians" challenge the Zionist political enterprise, particularly vis-à-vis the Arabs, the sociological critique focuses on Israel as a "settler society" and on the teleological Jewish assumptions of an Ashkenazi Labor pioneering elite, which sees in the founding of the Israeli state the culmination of Jewish history. See also the critique of Labor Zionism in Sternhell (1998).

7. The idea of "invention" tends to omit the social and institutional aspects of the nation—its mass, public culture; the role of historic territory; the new division of labor; the importance of national defense; the impact of the center and the framework of common laws—for the elements of cultural artifact and representation. Besides, "invention" is a term with a range of meanings, from "forgery" at one extreme to "recombination" (of existing elements) at the other; see Banks (1972).

8. And, while the upper clergy sided for the most part with the Ottoman authorities, the lower clergy were mainly supporters of the Greek revolt, especially in the Peloponnese; for them the Greek war of independence was continuous with and an expression of the long-standing hostility of Orthodox Christians to Muslim Turkish oppression. See Frazee (1969).

9. As we saw, Hobsbawm (1990, chap. 2) realized the problem. He criticized Gellner for his exclusive concern with a top-down approach but then went on to deny any connection between what he called "proto-national" communities, or bonds, and modern nationalisms, because

they have "no necessary connection with the unit of territorial political organisations" (ibid., 47) that we call modern nations. But such a criterion seems unnecessarily restrictive. It makes it difficult to explain the character, appeal, and historical role of nations and nationalisms for different strata of the population. In the end, Hobsbawm's explanation is overly instrumentalist and rationalist.

10. Only Benedict Anderson appears to have grasped the size of the problem. But his solution is curious. Instead of offering a historical and sociological explanation, he retreats into the idealist claim that people are prepared to die for the nation because, like the family, it is seen as a disinterested and solidary brotherhood, and so it alone can inspire love and sacrifice (Anderson 1991, 141–44). But even if this were true of either nation or family, people are rarely prepared to sacrifice themselves en masse for an abstract ideal, however disinterested, unless it is perceived to be linked to their individual needs, problems, and interests. As both Breuilly (1993) and Mosse (1976, 1994) demonstrate in their different ways, nationalism was ideally suited to combine collective ideals with individual needs and problems.

11. Where such approximations occur in a given culture area and are carried in the shared memories of ethnic communities, the premodern exemplum may provide a cultural resource for later generations or for other peoples in the same cultural tradition, as Hastings demonstrated of the Jews in the Christian tradition. But this is a matter that cannot be decided a priori; it requires empirical investigation over the *longue durée*.

12. For the Kalevala and the Finnish case, see Branch (1985, introduction) and for its influence, see Honko (1985). For the impact of nationalism on archaeology and the ethnic and nationalist interpretations of the archaeological record and its discoveries, see the essays in Diaz-Andreu and Champion (1996) and the analysis in Jones (1997).

13. Yet there was nothing new about this nostalgia for a golden age. As far back as the Neo-Sumerian Third Dynasty of Ur and the Bible's creation myth, as well as the poetry of Hesiod and Virgil, we find the same yearning for a lost age of ancestral purity, peace, and glory (see Armstrong 1982, chap. 2; Piggott 1985, chap. 4; and A. D. Smith 1986, chap. 3).

14. At one extreme are the large numbers of ethnic categories, named human groups sharing one or more elements of culture and linked to a particular terrain but with little sense of solidarity, few shared memories, and no ancestry myths; here we might cite the eighteenth-century Slovaks or Ukrainians. At the other extreme are the fully formed ethnic communities (*ethnies*), like the Poles and Sinhalese, with elaborate ancestry myths, shared memories, and a strong sense of solidarity. Some *ethnies* have remained relatively quiescent, like the Copts; others, like the Kurds and Tamils, are waging wars of national liberation. These are only some of the many variations in the fluid world of ethnicity and nationalism. (See A. D. Smith 1986, chap. 2; Eriksen 1993.)

15. Even in the earlier elite and middle-class nations, reference was often made to the needs of wider strata and their vernacular cultures, and

even the more aristocratic *ethnies* were based on communities of pre-sumed shared descent and common customs, as Reynolds (1984, chap. 8) showed for the *regna* of early medieval western Europe. See also A. D. Smith (1986, chap. 4).

16. Within each of these patterns there are significant variations. Per-haps the most important relates to the epoch of nation formation. For ex-ample, later attempts by aristocratic *ethnies* to incorporate culturally the population of "their" state encountered serious obstacles, as happened with the Tanzimat reforms by the Ottoman sultans or the Russification policies of the tsars in the nineteenth century; by that time, ethnic intelli-gentsias under the influence of nationalism and the example of the Anglo-French model tended to resist state homogenization and its "official na-tionalism" (see Anderson 1991, chap. 6; cf. Lewis 1968, and Hosking 1997). On the other hand, attempts by premodern *ethnies* to mobilize peo-ple and forge nations were often hampered, because they lacked the ideo-logical blueprint of nationalism and the skills of a secular intelligentsia (see Gouldner 1979).

17. This is why Armstrong (1992) distinguishes nations before 1800—that is, before nationalism—from those that emerged after this watershed. It is an important distinction, but Armstrong does not develop it. Unlike Hastings, I would regard nationalist theory as important in its own right, because of its universality in principle and its capacity for being disembed-ded from particular contexts. This allows nationalist ideology to be appro-priated across the globe, because it can be used to make sense of all kinds of circumstances through its ability to link past, present, and future (A. D. Smith 1991, chap. 4). As I have argued elsewhere, nationalism can be seen as a form of political archaeology, seeking out continuities in order to re-veal the ancient layering of nations and glossing over discontinuities. But nationalism is equally important as a secular form of "salvation drama": it posits a heroic myth of collective salvation through communal regenera-tion in the image of the golden age and by means of a sacred mission of the chosen community. (See Hutchinson 1987, chap. 1; A. D. Smith 1995a, 1999.)

18. We see the same use of Christian as well as classical myths and motifs in the monuments, memorials, and tombs of public commemo-rations documented by George Mosse (1990) for Western Europe, as well as in much of the history painting and sculpture of the eighteenth and nineteenth centuries, in the work of David and Ingres, Fuseli and Flax-man, Benjamin West and Canova, Goya and Delacroix, Burne-Jones and Rodin. See Rosenblum (1967, chap. 2), Honour (1968, chap. 3), and A. D. Smith (1993).

19. This is not to say there are no cultural traditions, like humanism and romanticism and social democracy on which Europeans cannot draw, nor that a limited economic and political union could not provide a stable framework for a *Europe des patries*. But this is to institutionalize nations and their nationalisms, not to transcend them. See the essays in Gowan and Anderson (1996) and A. D. Smith (1995b, chap. 5).

Bibliography

Acton, Lord. 1948. Nationality. In *Essays on freedom and power*. Glencoe, Ill.: Free Press.

Akenson, Donald. 1992. *God's Peoples: Covenant and land in South Africa, Israel, and Ulster*. Ithaca, N.Y.: Cornell University Press.

Akzin, Benjamin. 1964. *State and nation*. London: Hutchinson.

Alter, Peter. 1989. *Nationalism*. London: Peter Arnold.

Alty, J. H. 1982. Dorians and Ionians. *Journal of Hellenic Studies* 102: 1–14.

Anderson, Benedict. 1991. *Imagined communities: Reflections on the origins and spread of nationalism*. London: Verso Editions and New Left Books.

Armstrong, John. 1982. *Nations before nationalism*. Chapel Hill: University of North Carolina Press.

———. 1992. The autonomy of ethnic identity: Historic cleavages and nationality relations in the USSR. In *Thinking theoretically about Soviet nationalities*, edited by Alexander Motyl, 23–44. New York: Columbia University Press.

———. 1997. Religious nationalism and collective violence. In *Nations and Nationalism*. 3 (4): 597–606.

Assmann, Jan. 1997. *The Egyptian Moses: The memory of Egypt in Western monotheism*. Cambridge, Mass.: Harvard University Press.

Avery, Peter. 1965. *Modern Iran*. London: Ernest Benn.

Baker, Keith. 1988. *Inventing the French Revolution: Essays on French political culture in the eighteenth century*. Cambridge: Cambridge University Press.

Banks, Joe. 1972. *The sociology of social movements*. London: Macmillan.

Barnard, F. M. 1965. *Herder's social and political thought: From Enlightenment to nationalism*. Oxford: Clarendon Press.

———. 1983. National culture and political legitimacy. *Journal of the History of Ideas* 44: 231–53.

Baron, Salo. 1960. *Modern nationalism and religion*. New York: Meridian Books.

Barth, Fredrik, ed. 1969. *Ethnic groups and boundaries*. Boston: Little, Brown.

Baynes, Norman, and H. St. L. B. Moss, eds. 1969. *Byzantium: An introduction to East Roman civilisation*. Oxford: Oxford University Press.

Beaune, Colette. 1985. *Naissance de la nation française*. Paris: Editions Gallimard.

Beetham, David. 1974. *Max Weber and the theory of modern politics.* London: Allen and Unwin.

Berlin, Isaiah. 1976. *Vico and Herder.* London: Hogarth Press.

———. 1979. *Against the current.* London: Hogarth Press.

Bhabha, Homi, ed. 1990. *Nation and narration.* London and New York: Routledge.

Billig, Michael. 1995. *Banal nationalism.* London: Sage.

Bloch, Marc. 1961. *Feudal society.* 2 vols. London: Routledge and Kegan Paul.

Branch, Michael, ed. 1985. *Kalevala, the land of heroes.* Translated by W. F. Kirby. London: Athlone Press.

Brandon, S. G. F. 1967. *Jesus and the zealots.* Manchester: Manchester University Press.

Brass, Paul. 1979. Elite groups, symbol manipulation and ethnic identity among the Muslims of South Asia. In *Political identity in South Asia,* edited by David Taylor and Malcolm Yapp, 35–77. Dublin: Curzon Press.

———. 1991. *Ethnicity and nationalism.* London: Sage.

Bremmer, Ian, and Ray Taras, eds. 1993. *Nations and politics in the Soviet successor states.* Cambridge: Cambridge University Press.

Breton, Raymond. 1988. From ethnic to civic nationalism: English Canada and Quebec. *Ethnic and Racial Studies* 11 (1): 85–102.

Breuilly, John. 1993. *Nationalism and the state.* 2d ed. Manchester: Manchester University Press.

———. 1996a. Approaches to nationalism. In *Mapping the nation,* edited by Gopal Balakrishnan, 146–74. London and New York: Verso.

———. 1996b. *The formation of the first German nation state, 1800–1871.* Basingstoke, UK: Macmillan.

Brubaker, Rogers. 1992. *Citizenship and nationhood in France and Germany.* Cambridge, Mass.: Harvard University Press.

———. 1996. *Nationalism reframed: Nationhood and the national question in the new Europe.* Cambridge: Cambridge University Press.

Bruford, W. H. 1965. *Germany in the eighteenth century.* Cambridge: Cambridge University Press.

Cambridge History of Iran. 1983. Vol. 3, *The Seleucid, Parthian and Sassanian Periods,* edited by E. Yarshater. Cambridge: Cambridge University Press.

———. 1975. Vol. 4, *The period from the Arab invasion to the Saljuqs,* edited by R. N. Frye. Cambridge: Cambridge University Press.

Campbell, John, and Philip Sherrard. 1968. *Modern Greece.* London: Benn.

Carr, Edward. 1945. *Nationalism and after.* London: Oxford University Press.

Carras, C. 1983. *3000 Years of Greek identity: Myth or reality?* Athens: Domus Books.

Castles, Stephen, Bill Cope, Mary Kalantzis, and Michael Morrissey. 1988. *Mistaken identity: Multiculturalism and the demise of nationalism in Australia.* Sydney: Pluto Press.

Cauthen, Bruce. 1997. The myth of divine election and Afrikaner ethno-genesis. In *Myths and nationhood*, edited by Geoffrey Hosking and George Schöpflin, 107–31. London: Routledge.

Chatterjee, Partha. 1993. *The nation and its fragments*. Cambridge: Cambridge University Press.

Cobban, Alfred. [1945] 1969. *The nation-state and national self-determination*. Rev. ed., London: Collins.

Cohler, Anne. 1970. *Rousseau and nationalism*. New York: Basic Books.

Cohn, Norman. 1957. *The pursuit of the millennium*. London: Secker and Warburg.

Colley, Linda. 1992. *Britons: Forging the nation, 1707–1837*. New Haven, Conn.: Yale University Press.

Connor, Walker. 1984. *The national question in Marxist-Leninist theory and strategy*. Princeton, N.J.: Princeton University Press.

———. 1994. *Ethno-nationalism: The quest for understanding*. Princeton, N.J.: Princeton University Press.

Conversi, Daniele. 1998. *The Basques, the Catalans, and Spain: Alternative routes to nationalist mobilisation*. London: C. Hurst & Co.

Cottam, Richard. 1979. *Nationalism in Iran*. Pittsburgh: University of Pittsburgh Press.

Davis, Horace. 1967. *Nationalism and socialism: Marxist and Labor theories of nationalism*. London and New York: Monthly Review Press.

Davis, R. H. C. 1976. *The Normans and their myth*. London: Thames & Hudson.

Deutsch, Karl. 1966. *Nationalism and social communications*. 2d ed. Cambridge, Mass.: M.I.T. Press.

Diaz-Andreu, Margarita, and Timothy Champion, eds. 1996. *Nationalism and archaeology in Europe*. London: UCL Press.

Dinur, Ben-Zion. 1969. *Israel and the diaspora*. Philadelphia: Jewish Publication Society of America.

Doob, Leonard. 1964. *Patriotism and nationalism: Their psychological foundations*. New Haven, Conn.: Yale University Press.

Dunn, John. 1978. *Western political theory in the face of the future*. Cambridge: Cambridge University Press.

Eisenstadt, Shmuel. 1965. *Modernization: Protest and change*. Englewood Cliffs, N.J.: Prentice-Hall.

Eliade, Mircea. 1958. *Myths, dreams and mysteries*. Chicago and London: University of Chicago Press.

Eller, Jack, and Reed Coughlan. 1993. The poverty of primordialism: The demystification of ethnic attachments. *Ethnic and Racial Studies* 16 (2): 183–202.

Eriksen, Thomas. 1993. *Ethnicity and nationalism*. London and Boulder Colo.: Pluto Press.

Esman, Milton, ed. 1977. *Ethnic conflict in the Western world*. Ithaca, N.Y.: Cornell University Press.

Finley, Moses. 1986. *The use and abuse of history*. London: Hogarth Press.

Fishman, Joshua. 1980. Social theory and ethnography: Neglected perspectives on language and ethnicity in Eastern Europe. In *Ethnic diversity and conflict in Eastern Europe,* edited by Peter Sugar, 69–99. Santa Barbara, Calif.: ABC-Clio.

Florescano, Enrique. 1993. The creation of the Museo Nacional de Antropología of México and its scientific, educational and political purposes. In *Collecting the pre-Colombian past,* edited by Elisabeth Boone, 81–103. Washington, D.C.: Dumbarton Oaks Research Library and Collection.

Fondation Hardt. 1962. *Grecs et barbares, Entretiens sur l'antiquité classique.* Vol. 8. Geneva: Fondation Hardt.

Forde, Simon, Lesley Johnson, and Alan Murray, eds. 1995. *Concepts of national identity in the Middle Ages.* Leeds: University of Leeds, School of English.

Frazee, C. A. 1969. *The Orthodox church and independent Greece, 1821–52.* Cambridge: Cambridge University Press.

Frye, Richard. 1966. *The heritage of Persia.* New York: Mentor.

———, ed. 1975. *The period from the Arab invasion to the Saljuqs.* Vol. 4 of the *Cambridge History of Iran.* Cambridge: Cambridge University Press.

Geertz, Clifford. 1973. *The interpretation of cultures.* London: Fontana.

Gellner, Ernest. 1964. *Thought and change.* London: Weidenfeld and Nicolson.

———. 1983. *Nations and nationalism.* Oxford: Blackwell.

———. 1994. *Encounters with nationalism.* Oxford: Blackwell.

Gershoni, Israel, and Mark Jankowski. 1987. *Egypt, Islam and the Arabs: The search for Egyptian nationhood, 1900–1930.* New York and Oxford: Oxford University Press.

Gildea, Robert. 1994. *The Past in French History.* New Haven, Conn.: Yale University Press.

Gillingham, John. 1992. The beginnings of English imperialism. *Journal of Historical Sociology* 5: 392–409.

Gillis, John, ed. 1994. *Commemorations: The politics of national identity.* Princeton, N.J.: Princeton University Press.

Glazer, Nathan, and Daniel Moynihan, eds. 1975. *Ethnicity: theory and experience.* Cambridge, Mass.: Harvard University Press.

Gouldner, Alvin. 1979. *The rise of the intellectuals and the future of the new class.* London: Macmillan.

Gowan, Peter, and Perry Anderson, eds. 1996. *The question of Europe.* London and New York: Verso.

Greenfeld, Liah. 1992. *Nationalism: Five roads to modernity.* Cambridge, Mass.: Harvard University Press.

Grosby, Steven. 1991. Religion and nationality in antiquity. *European Journal of Sociology* 32: 229–65.

———. 1993. Kinship, territory and the nation in the historiography of ancient Israel. *Zeitschrift für die Alttestamentliche Wissenschaft* 105: 3–18.

———. 1994. The verdict of history: The inexpungeable tie of primordiality—a reply to Eller and Coughlan. *Ethnic and Racial Studies* 17 (1): 164–71.

———. 1995. Territoriality: The transcendental, primordial feature of modern societies. *Nations and Nationalism* 1 (2): 143–62.

———. 1997. Borders, territory and nationality in the ancient Near East and Armenia. *Journal of the Economic and Social History of the Orient* 40 (1): 1–29.

Guenée, Bernard. [1971] 1985. *States and rulers in later medieval Europe.* Translated by Juliet Vale. Oxford: Blackwell.

Guibernau, Montserrat. 1996. *Nationalisms: The nation-state and nationalism in the twentieth century.* Cambridge: Polity Press.

Gutierrez, Natividad. 1999. *The Culture of the Nation: The Ethnic Past and Official Nationalism in Twentieth Century Mexico.* Lincoln: University of Nebraska Press.

Gutmann, Amy, ed., 1994. *Multi-culturalism: Examining the politics of recognition.* Princeton, N.J.: Princeton University Press.

Hadas, Moses. 1950. National survival under Hellenistic and Roman imperialism. *Journal of the History of Ideas* 11: 131–39.

Haim, Sylvia, ed. 1962. *Arab nationalism: An anthology.* Berkeley and Los Angeles: University of California Press.

Hall, Edith. 1992. *Inventing the barbarian: Greek self-definition through tragedy.* Oxford: Clarendon Press.

Hall, John, ed. 1998. *The state of the nation: Ernest Gellner and the theory of nationalism.* Cambridge: Cambridge University Press.

Hastings, Adrian. 1997. *The construction of nationhood: Ethnicity, religion, and nationalism.* Cambridge: Cambridge University Press.

Hayes, Carlton. 1931. *The historical evolution of modern nationalism.* New York: Smith.

Herder, Johann. 1877–1913. *Sämmtliche Werke.* Edited by B. Suphan. Berlin: Weidmann.

Hertz, Frederick. 1944. *Nationality in history and politics.* London: Routledge and Kegan Paul.

Hertzberg, Arthur, ed. 1960. *The Zionist idea: A reader.* New York: Meridian Books.

Hobsbawm, Eric. 1990. *Nations and nationalism since 1780.* Cambridge: Cambridge University Press.

Hobsbawm, Eric, and Terence Ranger, eds. 1983. *The invention of tradition.* Cambridge: Cambridge University Press.

Honko, Lauri. 1985. The *Kalevala* Process. *Books from Finland* 19 (1): 16–23.

Honour, Hugh. 1968. *Neo-classicism.* Harmondsworth, UK: Penguin.

Hooson, David, ed. 1994. *Geography and national identity.* Cambridge, Mass., and Oxford: Blackwell.

Hosking, Geoffrey. 1997. *Russia: People and empire, 1552–1917.* London: Harper Collins.

Hosking, Geoffrey, and George Schöpflin, eds. 1997. *Myths and nationhood.* London: Routledge.

Hughes, Michael. 1988. *Nationalism and society: Germany, 1800–1945.* London: Edward Arnold.

Hutchinson, John. 1987. *The dynamics of cultural nationalism: The Gaelic revival and the creation of the Irish nation state.* London: Allen and Unwin.

———. 1994. *Modern nationalism.* London: Fontana.

Ichijo, Atsuko. 1998. Scotland and Europe: Scottish national identity and European integration. Ph.D. diss., University of London.

Ignatieff, Michael. 1993. *Blood and belonging: Journeys into the new nationalisms.* London: Chatto and Windus.

———. 1998. *The warrior's honour: Ethnic war and the modern consciousness.* London: Chatto and Windus.

Im Hof, Ulrich. 1991. *Mythos Schweiz: Identität-Nation-Geschichte, 1291–1991.* Zürich: Neue Verlag Zürcher Zeitung.

Johnson, Lesley. 1995. Imagining communities: Medieval and modern. In *Concepts of national identity in the Middle Ages,* edited by Simon Forde, Lesley Johnson, and Alan Murray, 1–19. Leeds: University of Leeds, School of English.

Jones, Sian. 1997. *The archaeology of ethnicity: Constructing identities in the past and the present.* London and New York: Routledge.

Juergensmeyer, Mark. 1993. *The new cold war? Religious nationalism confronts the secular state.* Berkeley and Los Angeles: University of California Press.

Just, Roger. 1989. The triumph of the *ethnos.* In *History and ethnicity,* edited by Elisabeth Tonkin, Maryon McDonald, and Malcolm Chapman, 71–88. London and New York: Routledge.

Kamenka, Eugene, ed. 1976. *Nationalism: The nature and evolution of an idea.* London: Edward Arnold.

Kantorowicz, E. H. 1951. *Pro patria mori* in medieval political thought. *American Historical Review* 56: 472–92.

Kapferer, Bruce. 1988. *Legends of people, myths of state: Violence, intolerance, and political culture in Sri Lanka and Australia.* Washington, D.C., and London: Smithsonian Institution.

Kaufmann, Eric, and Oliver Zimmer. 1998. In search of the authentic nation: Landscape and national identity in Canada and Switzerland. *Nations and Nationalism* 4 (4): 483–510.

Keddie, Nikki. 1981. *Roots of revolution: An interpretive history of modern Iran.* New Haven, Conn.: Yale University Press.

Kedourie, Elie. 1960. *Nationalism,* London: Hutchinson.

———, ed. 1971. *Nationalism in Asia and Africa.* London: Weidenfeld and Nicolson.

Kedourie, Sylvia, ed. 1998. *Elie Kedourie, CBE, FBA, 1926–92: History, philosophy, politics.* London and Portland, Oreg.: Frank Cass.

Kedward, Roderick. 1965. *The Dreyfus Affair.* London: Longman.

Kemilainen, Aira. 1964. *Nationalism: Problems concerning the word, the concept and classification.* Yvaskyla, Finland: Kustantajat Publishers.

Kitromilides, Paschalis. 1979. The dialectic of intolerance: Ideological dimensions of ethnic conflict. *Journal of the Hellenic Diaspora* 6 (4): 5–30.

———. 1989. 'Imagined communities' and the origins of the national question in the Balkans. *European History Quarterly* 19 (2): 149–92.

———. 1998. On the intellectual content of Greek nationalism: Paparrigopoulos, Byzantium, and the Great Idea. In *Byzantium and the modern Greek identity*, edited by David Ricks and Paul Magdalino. King's College, London: Centre for Hellenic Studies, Aldershot: Ashgate Publishing.

Klausner, Samuel. 1960. Why they chose Israel. *Archives de Sociologie des Religions* 9: 129–44.

Knoll, Paul. 1993. National consciousness in medieval Poland. *Ethnic Studies* 10 (1):65–84.

Kohn, Hans. 1940. The origins of English nationalism. *Journal of the History of Ideas* 1: 69–44.

———. 1955. *Nationalism: Its meaning and history*. New York: Van Nostrand.

———. 1957. *Nationalism and liberty: The Swiss example*. London: Macmillan.

———. 1960. *Pan-Slavism*. 2d ed. New York: Vintage Books.

———. 1961. *Prophets and peoples*. New York: Collier.

———. 1965. *The mind of Germany*. London: Macmillan.

———. [1944] 1967a. *The idea of nationalism*. 2d ed. New York: Collier-Macmillan.

———. 1967b. *Prelude to nation-states: The French and German experience, 1789–1815*. New York: Van Nostrand.

Koht, Halvdan. 1947. The dawn of nationalism in Europe. *American Historical Review* 52: 265–80.

Kreis, Georg. 1991. *Der Mythos von 1291: Zur Enstehung des schweizerischen Nationalfeiertags*. Basel: Friedrich Reinhardt Verlag.

Krejci, Yaroslav, and Viteslav Velimsky. 1981. *Ethnic and political nations in Europe*. London: Croom Helm.

Kushner, David. 1976. *The rise of Turkish nationalism*. London: Frank Cass.

Kymlicka, William. 1995. *Multicultural citizenship: A liberal theory of minority rights*. Oxford: Clarendon Press.

Lehmann, Jean-Pierre. 1982. *The roots of modern Japan*. London and Basingstoke: Macmillan.

Leith, J. A. 1965. *The idea of art as propaganda in France, 1750–99*. Toronto: University of Toronto Press.

Levi, Mario Attilio. 1965. *Political power in the ancient world*. Translated by J. Costello. London: Weidenfeld and Nicolson.

Lewis, Bernard. 1968. *The emergence of modern Turkey*. London: Oxford University Press.

———. 1970. *The Arabs in history*. 5th ed. London: Hutchinson & Co.

Llobera, Josep. 1994. *The God of modernity*. Oxford: Berg.

MacDougall, Hugh. 1982. *Racial myth in English history: Trojans, Teu-*

tons, and Anglo-Saxons. Montreal: Harvest House; Hanover, N.H.: University Press of New England.

Mango, Cyril. 1980. *Byzantium: The empire of the new Rome*. London: Weidenfeld and Nicolson.

Marcu, E. D. 1976. *Sixteenth century nationalism*. New York: Abaris Books.

McCrone, David. 1998. *The sociology of nationalism*. London and New York: Routledge.

McCulley, B. T. 1966. *English education and the origins of Indian nationalism*. Gloucester, Mass.: Smith.

McNeill, William. 1986. *Polyethnicity and national unity in world history*. Toronto: University of Toronto Press.

Mendels, Doron. 1992. *The rise and fall of Jewish nationalism*. New York: Doubleday.

Miles, Robert, ed. 1993. Migration and the new Europe. *Ethnic and Racial Studies* 16 (3): 459–562.

Miller, David. 1995. *On nationality*. Oxford: Oxford University Press.

Minogue, Kenneth. 1967. *Nationalism*. London: Batsford.

Morgan, Prys. 1983. From a death to a view: The hunt for the Welsh past in the Romantic period. In *The invention of tradition*, edited by Eric Hobsbawm and Terence Ranger, 43–100. Cambridge: Cambridge University Press.

Mosse, George. 1976. *The nationalisation of the masses*. Ithaca, N.Y.: Cornell University Press.

———. 1990. *Fallen soldiers*. Oxford and New York: Oxford University Press.

———. 1994. *Confronting the nation: Jewish and Western nationalisms*. Hanover, N.H.: University Press of New England/Brandeis University.

———. 1995. Racism and nationalism. *Nations and nationalism* 1 (2): 163–73.

Nora, Pierre, ed. 1984. *Les Lieux de memoire*. Vol. 1, *La République*. Paris: Gallimard.

———. 1986. *Les Lieux de memoire*. Vol. 2, *La Nation*. Paris: Gallimard.

O'Brien, Conor Cruse. 1988. *God-land: Reflections on religion and nationalism*. Cambridge, Mass.: Harvard University Press.

O'Leary, Brendan. 1996. Symposium on David Miller's "*On nationality*." *Nations and Nationalism* 2 (3): 409–51.

Palmer, R. R. 1940. The national idea in France before the Revolution. *Journal of the History of Ideas* 1: 95–111.

Pearson, Raymond. 1993. Fact, fantasy, fraud: Perceptions and projections of national revival. *Ethnic Studies* 10: 1–3, 43–64.

Peel, John. 1989. The cultural work of Yoruba ethno-genesis. In *History and ethnicity*, edited by Elisabeth Tonkin, Maryon McDonald, and Malcolm Chapman, 198–215. London and New York: Routledge.

Piggott, Stuart. 1985. *The Druids*. London: Thames and Hudson.

Pinson, Koppel, ed. 1960. *Nationalism and history: The writings of Simon Dubnow*. Philadelphia: Jewish Publication Society of America.

Pipes, Richard. 1977. *Russia under the old regime*, London: Peregrine Books.

Poliakov, Leon. 1974. *The Aryan myth*. New York: Basic Books.

Ram, Uri. 1995. Zionist historiography and the invention of modern Jewish nationhood: The case of Ben Zion Dinur. *History and Memory* 7: 91–124.

———. 1998. Postnationalist pasts: The case of Israel. *Social Science History* 22 (4): 513–45.

Reiss, H. S., ed. 1955. *The political thought of the German Romantics, 1793–1815*. Oxford: Blackwell.

Renan, Ernest. 1882. *Qu'est-ce qu'une nation?* Paris: Calmann-Levy.

Reynolds, Susan. 1983. Medieval *origines gentium* and the community of the realm. *History* 68: 375–90.

———. 1984. *Kingdoms and communities in Western Europe, 900–1300*. Oxford: Clarendon Press.

Reynolds, Vernon. 1980. Sociobiology and the idea of primordial discrimination. *Ethnic and Racial Studies* 3 (3): 303–15.

Robinson, Francis. 1979. Islam and Muslim separatism. In *Political Identity in South Asia*, edited by David Taylor and Malcolm Yapp, 78–112. Dublin: Curzon Press.

Rosdolsky, R. 1964. Friedrich Engels und das Problem der "Geschichtslosen Völker." *Archiv für Sozialgeschichte* 4: 87–282.

Rosenblum, Robert. 1967. *Transformations in late eighteenth century art*. Princeton, N.J.: Princeton University Press.

———. 1985. *Jean-Auguste-Dominique Ingres*. London: Thames and Hudson.

Roudometov, Victor. 1998. From *"Rum Millet"* to Greek nation: Enlightenment, secularisation, and national identity in Ottoman Balkan society, 1453–1821. *Journal of Modern Greek Studies* 16 (1): 11–48.

Rousseau, Jean-Jacques. 1915. *The political writings of Rousseau*. 2 vols. Edited by C. E. Vaughan. Cambridge: Cambridge University Press.

Sarkisyanz, Emanuel. 1964. *Buddhist backgrounds of the Burmese revolution*. The Hague: Nijhoff.

Saunders, J. J. 1978. *A history of medieval Islam*. London: Routledge and Kegan Paul.

Schöpflin, George. 1980. Nationality in the fabric of Yugoslav politics. *Survey* 25: 1–19.

Schwarzfuchs, Simon. 1979. *Napoleon, the Jews, and the Sanhedrin*. London, Boston and Henley: Routledge and Kegan Paul.

Seton-Watson, Hugh. 1977. *Nations and states*, London: Methuen.

Shafer, Boyd. 1955. *Nationalism: Myth and reality*. New York: Harcourt, Brace.

Shafir, Gershon. 1989. *Land, labor, and the origins of the Israeli-Palestinian conflict, 1882–1914*. Cambridge: Cambridge University Press.

Sherrard, Philip. 1959. *The Greek East and the Latin West: A study in the Christian tradition*. London: Oxford University Press.

Shils, Edward. 1957. Primordial, personal, sacred, and civil ties. *British Journal of Sociology* 7: 13–45.

———. 1995. Nation, nationality, nationalism, and civil society. *Nations and Nationalism* 1 (1): 93–118.

Shimoni, Gideon. 1995. *The Zionist ideology.* Hanover, N.H.: University Press of New England/Brandeis University Press.

Sluga, Glenda. 1998. Identity, gender, and the history of European nations and nationalisms. *Nations and Nationalism* 4 (1): 87–111.

Smith, Anthony D. 1981. *The ethnic revival in the modern world.* Cambridge: Cambridge University Press.

———. [1971] 1983. *Theories of nationalism.* 2d ed. London: Duckworth; New York: Holmes and Meier.

———. 1984. National identity and myths of ethnic descent. *Research in Social Movements, Conflict, and Change* 7: 95–130.

———. 1986. *The ethnic origins of nations.* Oxford: Blackwell.

———. 1989. The origins of nations. *Ethnic and Racial Studies* 12 (3): 340–67.

———. 1991. *National identity.* Harmondsworth, UK: Penguin.

———. 1992a. Chosen peoples: Why ethnic groups survive. *Ethnic and Racial Studies* 15 (3): 436–56.

———. 1992b. Nationalism and the historians. *International Journal of Comparative Sociology* 33 (1–2): 58–80.

———. 1993. Art and nationalism in Europe. In *De Onmacht van het Grote: Cultuur in Europa,* edited by J. C. H. Blom et al., 64–80. Amsterdam: Amsterdam University Press.

———. 1994. The problem of national identity: Ancient, medieval, and modern? *Ethnic and Racial Studies* 17 (3): 375–99.

———. 1995a. Gastronomy or geology? The role of nationalism in the reconstruction of nations. *Nations and Nationalism* 1 (1): 3–23.

———. 1995b. *Nations and nationalism in a global era.* Cambridge: Polity Press.

———. 1995c. Zionism and diaspora nationalism. *Israel Affairs* 2 (2): 1–19.

———. 1996a. Memory and modernity: Reflections on Ernest Gellner's theory of nationalism. *Nations and Nationalism* 2 (3): 371–88.

———. 1996b. The resurgence of nationalism? Myth and memory in the renewal of nations. *British Journal of Sociology* 47 (4): 575–98.

———. 1997a. The golden age and national renewal. In *Myths and nationhood,* edited by Geoffrey Hosking and George Schöpflin, 36–59. London: Routledge.

———. 1997b. Nations and ethnoscapes. *Oxford International Review* 8 (2): 11–18.

———. 1998. *Nationalism and modernism.* London and New York: Routledge.

———. 1999. Ethnic election and national destiny: Some religious origins of national ideals. *Nations and Nationalism* 5 (3): 331–55.

Smith, Donald, ed. 1974. *Religion and political modernization.* New Haven, Conn.: Yale University Press.

Snyder, Louis. 1954. *The meaning of nationalism.* New Brunswick, N.J.: Rutgers University Press.

Soysal, Yacemin. 1994. *Limits of citizenship: Migrants and post-national membership in Europe.* Chicago: University of Chicago Press.

Stern, Menahem. 1971. The Hasmonean revolt and its place in the history of Jewish society and religion. In *Jewish society through the ages,* edited by H. H. Ben-Sasson and S. Ettinger, 92–106. New York: Schocken Books.

Sternhell, Zeev. 1998. *The founding myths of Israel: Nationalism, socialism, and the making of the Jewish state.* Translated by David Maisel. Princeton, N.J.: Princeton University Press.

Suny, Ronald Grigor. 1993a. *Looking towards Ararat: Armenia in modern history.* Bloomington and Indianapolis: Indiana University Press.

———. 1993b. *The revenge of the past: Nationalism, revolution, and the collapse of the Soviet Union.* Stanford, Calif.: Stanford University Press.

Tamir, Yael. 1993. *Liberal nationalism.* Princeton, N.J.: Princeton University Press.

Tcherikover, Victor. 1970. *Hellenistic civilisation and the Jews.* New York: Athenaeum.

Thom, Martin. 1990. Tribes without nations: The ancient Germans and the history of modern France. In *Nation and narration,* edited by Homi Bhabha, 23–43. London and New York: Routledge.

Thompson, Leonard. 1985. *The political mythology of apartheid.* New Haven, Conn.: Yale University Press.

Tilly, Charles, ed. 1975. *The formation of national states in Western Europe.* Princeton, N.J.: Princeton University Press.

Tipton, Leon, ed. 1972. *Nationalism in the Middle Ages.* New York: Holt, Rinehart and Winston.

Tiryakian, Edward, and Ronald Rogowski, eds. 1985. *New nationalisms of the developed West.* Boston and London: Allen and Unwin.

Tivey, Leonard, ed. 1980. *The nation-state.* Oxford: Martin Robertson.

Tonkin, Elisabeth, Maryon McDonald, and Malcolm Chapman, eds. 1989. *History and ethnicity.* London and New York: Routledge.

Tønnesson, Stein, and Hans Antlov, eds. 1996. *Asian forms of the nation.* Cambridge: Cambridge University Press.

Trigger, B. G., B. J. Kemp, D. O'Connor, and A. B. Lloyd. 1983. *Egypt: A social history.* Cambridge: Cambridge University Press.

Tudor, Henry. 1972. *Political myth.* London: Pall Mall Press.

Tuveson, E. L. 1968. *Redeemer nation: The idea of America's millennial role.* Chicago: University of Chicago Press.

Van den Berghe, Pierre. 1978. Race and ethnicity: A sociobiological perspective. *Ethnic and Racial Studies* 1 (4): 401–11.

———. 1995. Does race matter? *Nations and Nationalism* 1 (3): 357–68.

Van der Veer, Peter. 1994. *Religious nationalism: Hindus and Muslims in India.* Berkeley: University of California Press.

Viroli, Maurizio. 1995. *For love of country.* Oxford: Clarendon Press.

Vital, David. 1975. *The origins of Zionism.* Oxford: Clarendon Press.

Walek-Czernecki, M. T. 1929. Le role de la nationalité dans l'histoire de l'antiquité. *Bulletin of the International Committee of the Historical Sciences* 2 (2): 305–20.

Weber, Max. 1947. *From Max Weber: Essays in sociology.* London: Routledge and Kegan Paul.

———. 1968. *Economy and society.* 3 vols. New York: Bedminster Press.

Webster, Bruce. 1997. *Medieval Scotland: The making of an identity.* Basingstoke, UK: Macmillan.

Wilmsen, Edwin, and Patrick McAllister, eds. 1996. *The politics of difference: Ethnic premises in a world of power.* Chicago: University of Chicago Press.

Wilson, J. A. 1951. *The burden of Egypt.* Chicago: University of Chicago Press.

Wiseman, D. J., ed. 1973. *Peoples of the Old Testament.* Oxford: Clarendon Press.

Yarshater, E., ed. 1983. *The Seleucid, Parthian, and Sassanian periods.* Vol. 3 of the *Cambridge History of Iran.* Cambridge: Cambridge University Press.

Zeitlin, Irving. 1988. *Jesus and the Judaism of his time.* Cambridge: Polity Press.

Zerubavel, Yael. 1995. *Recovered roots: Collective memory and the making of Israeli national tradition.* Chicago: University of Chicago Press.

Index

Page references in *italics* indicate a significant section on a particular subject in the text.